FOOTS

By the same author:
  Singing in the Dark (with Dan Wooding)

Footsteps of Love

BARRY TAYLOR

KINGSWAY PUBLICATIONS
EASTBOURNE

Unless otherwise indicated, biblical quotations are from the
New International Version © 1973, 1978, 1984 by the
International Bible Society

Cover design by Paul Clark

British Library Cataloguing in Publication Data

Taylor, Barry
Footsteps of love.
I. Title
242.8

ISBN 0 86065 989 5

Printed in Great Britain for
KINGSWAY PUBLICATIONS LTD
1 St Anne's Road, Eastbourne, E Sussex BN21 3UN by
Clays Ltd, St. Ives plc
Typeset by J&L Composition Ltd, Filey, North Yorkshire

Nobody has understood me. They think I'm a madman because I wanted to be a true Christian. They turned me out like a dog, saying that I was causing a scandal, because I tried to relieve the misery of the wretched. I don't know what I am going to do. Perhaps you are right, and I am idle and useless on this earth.

Vincent Van Gogh[1]

There are so many people to thank. Everyone we meet adds shape to our life in some way. But specifically:

Dave and Rod, who share with me the care of the church.

Pat, Brian and Michael, my Aussie mates.

John Smith, who challenges my thinking and helps me to see with eyes of compassion.

Our worship team at the church who bring me so much joy.

Cathy, my wife, who loves me and shows me so much of the character of Christ.

And finally, the one who lovingly calls us to follow in his footsteps.

Contents

Foreword

It's a real privilege to recommend the man and the
book. For the last twenty years I've been convinced
that there is one persistent question to be faced by
the church: shall we follow the religion of the
Pharisees or the religion of Jesus? Barry has grasped
the nettle with both hands and courageously
challenged both the secular world and the church to
take seriously the life-transforming path of Jesus.

Barry is extraordinarily suited to address the
subject, having seen the hollow pace of life without
faith and lasting values during his days of rock riot
on the road with AC/DC.

On the other hand, it has been my privilege and
great satisfaction to speak in his church and see the
marks of grace and love in the life and example of
Barry and his wife in intelligent and compassionate
service.

Everybody hates Pharisees and hypocrites, but
nobody ever admits to the label personally.
However, the Pharisee lurks in the shadows of most
men and women, whether religious or secular.

In their own world, the Pharisees of Jesus' day
didn't seem too bad from a conservative point of
view. They campaigned for standards in the

community. They saw prostitutes as enemies of morality and family. They prayed for society publicly, loudly and often. They gave between a tenth and a third of their income to God and charity. They never missed church (or synagogue) meetings. They believed in the total word-perfect inspiration of the Old Testament Torah. They believed that the study of God's book was the highest order of intellectual pursuit.

All of this stuff would get you membership in most churches. But Jesus said that for all that, the Pharisees had neglected what really matters: justice, mercy, faithfulness and, above all, love. Barry calls us clearly to follow Jesus and not mere moral platitudes and legalistic forms of institutional religion.

This warm, challenging book is long overdue, and I know of few more suited than Barry to write it.

It is a thorough, well researched, intelligent and deeply concerned statement. I'm not just writing the foreword—I'm going to be carrying copies to pass on wherever I go.

John Smith
Melbourne, Australia

Introduction

> We constantly change the world, even by our inaction. Let us change it responsibly (Benjamin Franklin).[2]

> Let us not waste our time in idle discourse. Let us do something while we have the chance. It's not every day that we are needed, nor indeed that we are personally needed. Others would meet the case well, if not better. To all mankind they were addressed, those cries for help still ringing in our ears. But at this place, at this moment of time, all mankind is us, whether we like it or not . . . What are we doing here? That is the question (Samuel Beckett).[3]

In the eighteenth century, England was a terrible place. Christianity slept on while the nation became darker. Piety and morality thundered from the pulpits but never succeeded in impacting the community. Darkness was everywhere; it permeated every level of society from the royal courts to the poverty-stricken streets of London. It was a gross, thick, religious and moral darkness; a darkness, as Bishop J. C. Ryle wrote, 'that might be felt'.

Drunkenness was rampant, marauding gangs ruled the streets, no one was safe. A hundred and sixty

11

crimes were punishable by the death penalty. Hangings were a daily spectacle. The prison system was a nightmare. Young children who were caught stealing bread to stave off starvation were arrested and thrown into cells with the most hardened of violent criminals.

The pastimes of eighteenth-century England were violent and immoral. Bear-baiting and cock fighting were the sports of the wealthy. The theatre was coarse and immoral. All kinds of sexual sin were socially acceptable. Religion was tolerated, but had degenerated into form without power, and religious fervour was disdained.

Yet within an incredibly short period of time all heaven was let loose in Britain as the Wesleys and Whitefield spearheaded a massive religious awakening.

One of the great heresies of our time must surely be that in our world one person cannot make a difference. I don't believe that at all. One man, one woman, one group of individuals can make a tremendous difference and have significant impact on our lives and ways of living. The list is endless: Thomas Edison, Alexander Graham Bell, Louis Pasteur, and so on. Our history is full of people, ordinary people, who realised that with the courage of their conviction they could make a difference, despite conventional wisdom.

On a mountainside, hundreds of years ago, a man sat with his friends and laid an outrageous plan before them. In essence he said, 'You have no power, no influence, no social or political connections, no organisation, no credentials, no finances, but I want you to go to the whole world and tell everyone about me and my kingdom. In fact, I want you to challenge all existing religious thought in every culture with the story of my kingdom.'

They did it. In fact they were accused of turning the world upside down (Acts 17:6).

I believe that our world is ready to be turned upside down once again. It needs more than a clinical presentation of life as we Christians see it. The world needs an encounter with Jesus Christ himself. That can only happen through his church. The church following in his footsteps, being transformed into his likeness by the Spirit of the living God.

The challenge of impacting our culture is tremendous. Our world is incredibly advanced in technology, and at times our message seems somewhat lacking; a brown paper bag among brightly coloured and beautifully decorated boxes. The tendency is often to compete with the glamour and the glitter of our world, trying to prove that Christians have everything the world has and more. We will never be able to 'out-glitter' the world, and I am not so sure that that is the calling anyway.

'The Son of Man did not come to be served, but to serve, and to give his life as a ransom for many' (Mk 10:45). The essence of following Jesus is understanding that our task is not to compete with the spirit of our world but to serve people with love. I believe that God is calling his church to rediscover her true call and destiny to learn the spirit of servanthood: the manner, method and attitude of living that must compel us as a people. That attitude towards life is nowhere better modelled for us than in the life of Christ, who left the majesty and glory of heaven's throne, laying aside his deity and becoming not just a man but a servant; a servant to all mankind.

God, who is not human, became like us so that we could understand what he is like. He crossed the chasm between the created and their creator, and he did it by servanthood. The call of Christ to his disciples throughout the ages has been: 'Follow me.' To follow him is ultimately to allow his life to flow forth from our lives.

1

Give Me Something to Believe in

Everybody has a hungry heart (Bruce Springsteen).

You cannot set a tepid Christianity beside a scorching paganism (Ravi Zacharias).

. . . When he saw the crowds, he had compassion on them, because they were harassed and helpless, like sheep without a shepherd. Then he said to his disciples, 'The harvest is plentiful but the workers are few. Ask the Lord of the harvest, therefore, to send out workers into his harvest field' (Jesus—Mt 9:36–38).

We all have a set of assumptions about life, what it means, what is important. Those assumptions colour what we say, think and do.

To most Americans freedom would be, perhaps, one of their most deeply held values. The value and sense of freedom determines much of the Americans' response to the world around them. They take deep offence at the idea of infringing a human being's rights or limiting basic human freedom. However, most Americans would have differing opinions about what freedom is. To many Americans, freedom means 'the freedom to'. The freedom to make the most of life; the freedom to speak without fear; the freedom to live where one chooses;

15

the freedom to do whatever one wants with one's life, to fulfil one's heart's desires, and the freedom 'to make it', to fulfil the American Dream.

To other Americans, the idea of freedom is 'freedom from'. The freedom from having ideas or values forced upon them or being free from absolute authorities or from conformity to family or community. Ultimately, the freedom to be left alone to their own devices.

If we were to ask a group of Christians what it means to be a Christian, to be part of the church, we would discover many differing opinions and assumptions. It's a little like the Americans' interpretation of what freedom means. Some Christians believe that their faith removes them from the harshness and brokenness of our world and they retreat into ivory towers, perfecting their theology with little regard for the world around them. Other believers interpret things differently. They see their faith as the means by which they can serve their God, but also their fellow man.

What is important for us, as the church, is that our assumptions about life, our values and choices, are in line with the way God looks at the world, and that what we say and do and think about our world is shaped by him.

The great challenge of the church throughout its history has been to remain 'in this world but not of it'. More often than not, the church seems to have taken on a belated pale reflection of the dominant social mood of the hour.

The Bible is full of the stories of the prophets who came again and again to the people of God; a people who continually seemed to lose sight of what was important and as they became affected by and integrated into the cultures around them, forgot their destiny and purpose. The task of the prophet was to remind the people and call them back to their heavenly Father to renew their vision and redefine their pespectives about life and how they were to relate to the world around them.

Quite often, the people the prophets spoke to were maintaining what they regarded as a strong relationship with their God, but the prophets would always challenge them to a deeper interpretation of their relationship—that the God whom they served was not looking so much for outward form and ritual as he was for a people so in touch with his heart that they became willing vessels in his hands to accomplish his purposes on the earth.

How we look at and relate to the world as Christians is extremely important. It is so easy to look at the world through religious eyes and point out all its faults and failures, its gross darkness and sin, and dispassionately pass judgement. However, if we are to impact our world and see a generation come to Christ, then we need to do much more than simply offer religious judgements.

'When he saw the crowds, he had compassion on them, because they were harassed and helpless, like sheep without a shepherd. Then he said to his disciples, "The harvest is plentiful but the workers are few. Ask the Lord of the harvest, therefore, to send out workers into his harvest field"' (Mt 9:36–38). When Jesus looked at the world, he was wounded in his heart. He was deeply moved as he looked about him and saw the powerlessness and helplessness of humanity apart from God. Out of concern for the people, he called his disciples to him and challenged them to a new attitude—an

attitude that flew in the face of religious manner-
isms. In Jesus' day, the bulk of religious leaders
prided themselves on their distance and separation
from the world around them. For the most ardent
followers of God, even to brush past someone whose
relationship with God was less than perfect meant
that they became unclean. Distance from 'sinners',
therefore, was of high priority. The new attitude
that Jesus called his disciples to was a harvest attitude. It was a call to make themselves available to go
out and reap a harvest of humanity in need and
suffering.

It begins with the eyes. The Bible records Jesus so
often moved by the things he saw: the emptiness of
human lives devoid of relationship with God. If we
don't see as he saw, we won't feel what he felt, and if
we don't feel as he felt, we will never be able to
communicate with our world as he did with his.
Jesus saw people as they might be. Many of those he
called to follow him were sketchy in their
credentials. They had bad attitudes, limited
potential. They were people who tended to cave in
with the advent of pressure, but he saw something in
them that no one else could see. He knew that the
worst could become the best and lives could be
transformed.

We must look at the world with the transforming
eyes of the gospel and see what it could become
under the reign of God's kingdom.

The societies of our world are disintegrating.
Some sociologists contend that we have come to the
end of human history. Their theory is that human
history is made up of people gathering around great
ideas; ideas which fire the imagination and cause
people to gather together and join their hearts in

order to live out those ideas. Their view is that the world has run out of great ideas and all the future holds is an unravelling of our societies. As you look around the world, there appears to be some substance to their opinion. The collapse of Socialism, one of 'the great ideas' of the century, has left millions of people in absolute despair and fear as they struggle to make sense of life now that their dreamworld has collapsed.

Our society too is struggling to keep its head above water. Western society with all of its technology and creature comforts is at present being exposed as a less-than-perfect means to live out life with purpose and destiny.

It has been said that the more a man has in his own heart, the less he will have need for things from the outside. That excessive need for stimulus and support from outside sources is evidence that points towards the bankruptcy of the human heart. Our own society and its inordinate desire for every form of distraction is proof that the inner life of modern man is in serious trouble. People seem unable to live a day without the stimulation which our society brings them. There seems to be an almost desperate drive to fill our lives with every conceivable form of entertainment. We spend millions of pounds on every kind of stimulant from drugs and alcohol to movies and concerts, and it never seems to be enough. We are, quite possibly, the most entertained generation in the history of the world, and yet emptiness and shallowness pervade our culture. Decay has penetrated every level of society. Having turned our backs on God and released ourselves from the pressure of absolutes and morality, we have descended into a numbness that affects us all.

The luxuries of our society never satisfy. They simply serve as reminders that there are more things to be had.

> The pursuit of material things in the affluent Western world has not brought the promised paradise on earth. Instead, it throws into the clearest, coldest light, the spiritual, ethical and philosophical hunger of mankind. It is this hunger which remains unsatisfied in the affluent society. Increase in goods doesn't bring with it an increased sense of life worth living . . . Affluence does not seem to increase a care for things worth caring for (Charles Birch).[4]

With all of the 'stuff' that our culture brings us, it has been unable to satisfy the depth of the human heart.

> This is what the Lord says: 'Cursed is the one who trusts in man, who depends on flesh for his strength and whose heart turns away from the Lord. He will be like a bush in the wastelands; he will not see prosperity when it comes. He will dwell in the parched places of the desert, in a salt land where no-one lives' (Jer 17:5–6).

That describes our culture. In the midst of incredible prosperity in world terms, there is still deadness. The imagery that Jeremiah paints is one of abandonment. The man or the society that abandons God is itself abandoned. It symbolises that when a heart moves away from God, its source of well-being disappears. The society which has abandoned itself to supposed happiness and freedom has found itself in bondage and misery.

There is a growing awareness of the emptiness of materialism in much of twentieth-century life. There is a growing hunger among the peoples of the world, a rising cry for transcendence, for God, as more and more people become aware of the hollowness of society, and many more discover that there is not enough variety in the world to silence the cry and the need of the human spirit. There is talk, even among secular trend forecasters, of global religious awakenings and renewed interest in things spiritual. Mankind is longing for something real and tangible.

> When people believe 'the time is at hand', they typically cluster into small groups around colourful, eccentric leaders. Echoing past movements, millions today are attracted to the unorthodox ends of the religious spectrum: from New Age channellers, to 'speaking in tongues' charismatics, to scandal-prone TV preachers.
> The bond we share today with the people of past millennial eras is the sense of living in a time of enormous change. The last time the United States experienced such a deeply religious period was during the nineteenth century, when the country's economy changed from agriculture to industry. That century witnessed the creation of several major made-in-America religions: Mormon, Adventist, Jehovah's Witness, and Christian Scientist, along with the rise of the Transcendentalists and the popularity of spiritualism.[5]

'Give me something to believe in,' sang the rock group Poison in one of their hits. While they do not claim to speak for all of their peers, there is a sense of identification with their cry. The resurgence of rock songs and films that deal with the reality of human life and experience points, I believe, to the issues of our time; that while lives have been made more comfortable, nothing has been able to fill the gap in the human heart.

Jesus saw a people lost, living lives without meaning, and that sight evoked great emotion within his heart. He was moved with compassion. The sight of people without shape or direction caused him to gather his friends and share with them his deep desire to see people transformed by relationship with God. 'Now when he saw the crowds, he went up on a mountainside and sat down. His disciples came to him, and he began to teach them, saying: "Blessed are the poor in spirit, for theirs is the kingdom of heaven . . ."' (Mt 5:1–3).

Jesus came to a world made for so much more than it was given to. He understood that man was created for relationship with God, and the essence of his life and teaching was to demonstrate what humanity should look like when it rediscovers its Maker.

It was the 'seeing' of the multitudes that prompted what is still regarded as the most profound of the teachings of Jesus, the Sermon on the Mount. Many great scholars have dissected the teachings and presented the profound truths that Jesus gave on that hillside, with remarkable wisdom and insight. I do not feel capable of fully exegeting this remarkable portion of Scripture, but I do have a sense that when Jesus gave this, it was to capture what God intended man to be in the world.

Jeremiah's imagery of man, surrounded by wealth, yet characterised by deadness because he has abandoned his God, is in stark contrast to the picture of man Jesus paints. His is a picture of a totally different world. A world in which poverty of spirit is celebrated. To surround ourselves with the things of this world not only erases a sense of eternity, but also our ability to relate fully with each other, because the things which we possess ultimately become dividing walls between us all, creating class, bigotry and many other destructive characteristics that poison our world. Jesus calls us to be big enough to sit with him and mourn with him over the condition of a world made for love and relationship but given to so much else. He contrasts the self-indulgent, self-seeking spirit with the longing for a different world. He promises comfort to those willing to carry, in their own hearts, the woundedness of their own generation. He asks the question, 'Do you like the way the world is?' If not, then can you cry, 'Your kingdom come, your will be done on earth, in our world today, as it is in heaven'?

2

The Kingdom Is at Hand

Theology should not begin with an intellectual discussion about Christian doctrine or propositional truth, which is then applied to contemporary problems. Theology should begin with a commitment to change an unjust society into a just one.[6]

'Master, it is good for us to be here. Let us put up three shelters—one for you, one for Moses and one for Elijah.' (He did not know what he was saying.) (Lk 9:33).

Our task is to look at the world around us and see the tremendous opportunity God has given to us. As our world struggles to make sense of life, to find meaning, we who are the people of God have the answer. The world does not need another global religion. It needs to encounter Jesus, the only one who can bring man to God. It will only encounter Jesus through us.

If our effectiveness as Christians in the modern world is based upon our view of the world, it also holds true that how we are seen is vital to the futherance of Christ's kingdom. The message we proclaim has no credibility apart from its visibility. The proclaimer is an inseparable part of the message he proclaims.

Peter Kuzmic, a Yugoslav Christian leader, has said, 'Our basic need is not better methodology, but more authenticity. The answer to the question of world evangelism, "How shall they hear?" is inextricably linked to the question "What shall they see?"'

In a world which trusts that which can be handled by the senses, our task is to make Christ visible to a world for whom he is invisible. We must bring vision to the world—vision of another kingdom—to show and tell how life was meant to be. That means not only speaking words, but demonstrating Christ's love and the hope that he brings to a broken world.

'The kingdom of heaven is at hand' were the words that Jesus declared as he embarked on his ministry. He proceeded to proclaim it, not by words alone but by his very actions, bringing wholeness to the needs of society. To a world where religion was complex with form, ritual and enforced observances, Jesus took off the wrappers and invited a frail and bewildered humanity to come and look God in the face.

I must tell you, with evangelists it is the same as with artists. An old academic school full of tyrannical men who wear prejudice and convention. May God give us the grace to face the true and full content of the gospel of Jesus (Vincent Van Gogh).

In the Gospel of Mark, Jesus encounters a leprous man desperate for help. 'If you are willing, you can make me clean,' he said to Jesus. Jesus' response was to reach out compassionately and touch the man. To a man outcast by his disease, that touch must have meant almost as much as the cure. It is the world

that is touched by the love of Christ through the
church that will respond to the message we declare.

In Luke 9, we come across a profound religious
experience. Jesus had been talking about his death
and resurrection—things that his disciples hadn't
fully grasped. He invited three of his friends to
climb a mountain and pray with him. As Jesus
prayed, his face changed and his clothes began to
shine, and two figures from Israel's past showed
up—Moses and Elijah. Jesus' disciples had been
sleeping but this woke them up. When it was over,
Peter immediately wanted to institutionalise the
moment. He told Jesus that it was a really good idea
to stay there, build some chapels and enjoy the
mountain-top experience. He perhaps wanted to
create a retreat centre and hang on to the religious
experience so that it wouldn't fade away. Jesus
didn't reply, but a cloud showed up and God was in
it and he did the talking. 'Listen to him' was the
essence of God's word to the disciples, telling words
considering that Jesus had basically been speaking
of a gruesome future for himself.

Many people turn to religions that offer a sense of
peace and retreat from the world. However, the
symbol of the church is not a shelter on the side of a
mountain, but a bloody cross on a garbage heap; a
symbol of confrontation with evil. Being a Christian
is not about retreating from the ugliness and
brokenness of the world. Jesus didn't want to stay on
the mountainside because he had a destiny on the
cross. Even in the church, we can become consumed
with ourselves, and our religion can degenerate into
a self-serving practice—but that is not the purpose
of God for us.

Immediately Jesus and the disciples came down

from the mountain, they were met by a large crowd, and in that crowd was a man who begged Jesus to help his demonised son. That is what the church is all about. The presence of God that we encounter on the mountain-top is so that there might be an empowering to shed the love and power of God upon those who are broken. It was the world at the bottom of the mountain that Jesus came for. That same world must hear our message, but also see our lives. To be a Christian is all about confronting the evil that destroys by taking the compassionate, broken heart of God wherever circumstances demand.

Jesus calls us to follow him. That means more than simply following a belief system or holding to orthodox doctrine. It means being willing to walk where he walked, to do as he did and to demonstrate his love to our world. John said that we can know who the children of God are because they love to do what is right and love their brothers (1 Jn 3:10).

There was something compelling about Jesus; something that made ordinary people sit up and take notice. More than ever, our world needs to encounter Jesus.

3

Different to Make a Difference

When love comes to town, I'm gonna catch that flame (U2, 'When Love Comes to Town').

Now the tax collectors and 'sinners' were all gathering around to hear him. But the Pharisees and the teachers of the law muttered, 'This man welcomes sinners, and eats with them' (Lk 15:1–2).

What kind of man is this? Even the winds and the waves obey him! (Mt 8:27).

What kind of person was Jesus? If we are to represent him honestly in the earth, then we have to examine that question.

In the year 1514, a story was published in Italy. It claimed to be a description of Jesus by a man who was said to have been the Roman Procurator of Judea before or after Pontius Pilate. The book described Jesus and had an obvious effect on artists' renderings of him at that time.

He is a tall man, well shaped and of an amiable and reverend aspect; his hair is of a colour that can hardly be matched, falling into graceful curls ... parted on the crown of his head, running as a stream to the front after the fashion of the Nazarites; his forehead high, large and imposing; his cheeks without spot or wrinkle, beautiful with a lovely red; his nose and mouth formed with exquisite symmetry; his beard, and of a colour suitable to his hair, reaching below his chin and parted in the middle like a fork; his eyes bright blue, clear and serene . . . .[7]

In the next paragraph of the book, there appears a statement which seems to have had a profound impact on the church. It reads: 'No man has seen him laugh.'

Jesus was fully God and fully man, but how could he be if laughter was not a part of his life? To laugh is to be human. While it is certainly true that Jesus was a man of sorrows and acquainted with grief, he was also the man who turned water into wine, welcomed children and refused to bow to the pressure of his disciples to send the crowds away. In fact Jesus' reputation among his contemporaries was not that of a reserved, stern and unapproachable religious man. He was condemned for being a bit of a glutton and an imbiber of alcohol, and he was welcomed into the homes of sinners and was glad to attend. These are not the characteristics of a man who never smiled. The Gospels are full of the range of Jesus' emotion: his compassion and care, his tears for the city of Jerusalem, but also for his friend Lazarus, who had died. It is safe to say that if he displayed these emotions, then as a man he must have surely smiled.

Much of the residue left on the world by the church doesn't really represent Jesus. In our attempts to protect and promote Jesus' divinity from the many onslaughts it has received, I think we have tended to downplay his humanity. But it was his unique humanness that made him accessible. This is the man whom tax collectors and all kinds of social outcasts gladly listened to.

We have to take off our religious eyes when we look at Jesus in Scripture. The great difference between Jesus and his religious contemporaries, was the way in which he related to the world around him. Even though he lived in a small insignificant town in Galilee, he understood the realities of human life, tragedy, hopelessness, death and sickness. Isaiah said it well: 'He was despised and rejected by men, a man of sorrows, and familiar with suffering' (Is 53:3).

Galilee was a wealthy province. However, the Galileans were treated with suspicion by their southern relatives. They were regarded as un-educated peasants without manners and who spoke with bad accents. They were also regarded as not very religious.

The bulk of Jesus' life was spent in relative isolation, consumed with the realities of first-century Jewish village life. Rather than being removed from real life into the hallowed halls of religious learning, Jesus lived out his life in much the same way as the people he came to reach. He was in essence a common man, a man of the people. It was his earthiness that made him so appealing to the common people.

There is a unique story in the Bible about a wealthy tax collector called Zacchaeus; a short man so desperate to see Jesus that he climbed up a tree to catch a glimpse as Jesus walked by. Tax collectors were an interesting group. They were despised by their peers because they had willingly sacrificed family and societal ties for the sake of personal gain. They were looked upon with complete scorn by the

Jews and treated with contempt by the Romans. They weren't allowed to testify in court and were regarded, basically, as traitors. Yet this man, a chief tax collector, wanted to hear this teacher called Jesus. Why? Perhaps because he was different. Here was a Rabbi with twelve friends, and at least one of them was a tax collector as well. He was a Jewish leader who defied the culture in which he lived—a teacher who made friends with tax collectors. If we are to follow Jesus, we will also have to follow his pattern and defy our social groupings.

Zacchaeus wanted to see Jesus because he expressed the father heart of God to all mankind. As Jesus came along with a crowd, he stopped under Zacchaeus' tree and invited himself to dinner. Jesus wanted to dine with a non-person. In every culture we eat with our family and friends, and God wants everybody to dine at his table.

Zacchaeus was not a good man, as we've already said. In being a tax collector he had made up his mind to do something that would make him an outcast. When Jesus did this to Zacchaeus, the crowd did what people can always do so easily—they criticised. They began to wonder what kind of religious man Jesus was. They didn't even seem to be too happy with the idea that possibly, for the first time in his life, this man was willing to change his agenda and talk with Jesus.

In his desire to reach the outcast, Jesus continually brought his own reputation under scrutiny. He was criticised for being a glutton and a drunk—not very good credentials for a religious teacher. However, Jesus didn't care about his reputation. He understood that the kingdom of heaven is about redemption, and therefore he was willing to go where no self-seeking religious leader would go.

The God we serve was willing to put his reputation at stake, walking into the homes and lives of
the unlovely, and instead of writing them off, he was
willing to look beyond the outside, no matter how
dirty, and introduce the caring heart of God. If we
are to follow Jesus, we too must be prepared to put
our reputations on the line.

The Apostle Paul said it best: 'But whatever was to
my profit I now consider loss for the sake of Christ.
What is more, I consider everything a loss compared
to the surpassing greatness of knowing Christ Jesus
my Lord, for whose sake I have lost all things. I
consider them rubbish, that I may gain Christ and
be found in him' (Phil 3:7–9).

Jesus' relationship with the dregs of society was a
source of constant antagonism to the Pharisees. The
mere fact that he spoke with people like this was
enough for them to discount him as a true religious
leader, but eating with them and surrounding
himself with such people was almost too much for
them to handle.

Their religion was different. It was the nature of
Jesus to be given to people. The nature of the
religious was to be given to their belief system and
structure: 'At that time Jesus went through the
cornfields on the Sabbath. His disciples were hungry
and began to pick some ears of corn and eat them.
When the Pharisees saw this, they said to him,
"Look! Your disciples are doing what is unlawful on
the Sabbath"' (Mt 12:1–2).

The Pharisees suffered not from hardening of the
arteries, but with hardening of the categories! Their
structure became more important than people. It
made them separate from other people. Their faith
became both a barrier and a barometer by which

they judged others. They prided themselves on their relationship with God and they despised anyone else who failed to meet their very high standards.

Interestingly enough, the things they gave themselves to would not seem out of place in most churches today: prayer, evangelising, memorising Scripture, the making of disciples, fasting and giving. It was not so much the things they did as the attitude in which they were done.

Jesus' anger was most often directed against those who remained and developed self-serving institutions; against those who had lost sight of their purpose and calling and ceased to be servants. Jesus continually challenged their interpretation of the law and put it back into perspective. To the Pharisees, 'Remember the Sabbath' had become an institutional policy. Jesus reminded them that when God made the Sabbath, he made it for man and not vice versa. The religion of the Pharisees had reached a place where the very thing given and designed to liberate men (the law of God) was now the tool by which men were being destroyed. Pharisaism has never been on the cutting edge of what God is doing in the world.

The Pharisees and some of the teachers of the law who had come from Jerusalem gathered round Jesus and saw some of his disciples eating food with 'unclean'— that is, ceremonially unwashed—hands. (The Pharisees and all the Jews do not eat unless they give their hands a ceremonial washing, holding to the tradition of the elders. When they come from the market-place they do not eat unless they wash. And they observe many other traditions, such as the washing of cups, pitchers and kettles.)

So the Pharisees and teachers of the law asked Jesus, 'Why don't your disciples live according to the tradition of the elders instead of eating their food with "unclean" hands?'

He replied, 'Isaiah was right when he prophesied about you hypocrites; as it is written: "These people honour me with their lips, but their hearts are far from me. They worship me in vain; their teachings are but rules taught by men"' (Mk 7:1–7).

The Pharisees are great people to highlight when it comes to dealing with the issue of religiousness. However, at the root of their legalism was an honest and intense attempt to centre their lives on God. What had gone wrong is that they had become side-tracked with all the things associated with their faith. What began as a celebration of life with God, had killed the life of God in them; they became victims of their own traditions. In fact, the irony was that their traditions, which were designed to lead them to God, had driven a wedge between them and him. Their conscientiousness descended into pettiness and they began to place equal importance on observing both their man-made traditions and their God-given commands. Ultimately, their human traditions left them with no time to observe fully the commandments of God. Their religion had become idolatrous in its self-centredness and the exactness with which they attempted to observe their commands became the source of judgement towards others.

In quoting Isaiah, Jesus reminded them that the real issue is not in outward observance but in real relationship with God. Jesus went on to talk about the heart (vv. 14–23). Without the heart, no religious act can be complete. That is why Paul

contrasted love with all other religious acts in
1 Corinthians 13. Through many of his other letters
Paul battled with the tendency among people to
return to externals. Jesus also said that it is very easy
to enter into all kinds of sins which bring death,
while still fulfilling religious traditions with false
piety. He continually reminded the Pharisees of the
importance of keeping observances in their proper
places; they were never as important as the issues of
the heart. Unfortunately, the Pharisees found great
reward in the observances they performed so
diligently. They received notoriety, honour and
recognition for their religion, but they were also
regarded with scorn by those who failed to live up to
their standards.

Jesus emphasised continually the importance of
heart relationship with God. Perhaps one of the
most telling stories of this is the simple parable that
Jesus told in Luke 18 of two men going to the
temple to pray. The story tells of two men who each
stood apart from everyone else, but for different
reasons. The Pharisee stood apart because he was
self-righteous and despised other people. 'The
Pharisee stood apart by himself and prayed' (Lk
18:11, GNB).

In Jewish culture, those who kept the law in a
strict fashion were known as 'associates'; those who
did not were called 'people of the land'. In the eyes
of a Pharisee the most obvious candidate to be
classified as a person of the land would have been a
tax collector. There was also a particular type of
uncleanness that a Pharisee could contract by sitting
on, riding or even leaning against something
unclean. To become unclean was a horrifying thing
for a Pharisee. His state of cleanness before God was

of utmost importance to him, so rather than compromise that state he would stand apart, aloof. His standing apart was symbolic of his relationship to the rest of society. Here was a man who did not have dirt under his fingernails or mud on his clothing. His prayer reveals a lot about him. He was standing apart in case he became defiled by the uncleanness around him. He was a man who prided himself on his more-than-perfect observation of his religion.

He unleashed a ruthless attack on the other man in the story, the tax collector, who had also come to pray: 'God, I thank you that I am not like all other men—robbers, evildoers, adulterers—or even like this tax collector. I fast twice a week and give a tenth of all I get' (Lk 18:11–12). His 'prayer' was based on preconceived notions formed by his own righteousness, which he then proceeded to declare to the assembled listeners. He claimed to tithe on all that he gained, which was more than the law required, and was an obvious statement of his over-estimated sense of self-importance before God. His condemnation of the tax collector stands in stark contrast to the broken, humble man who stood some distance from the rest of the assembled worshippers. The Pharisees were always blinded by their preconceptions. People were put into boxes based upon their assessments of them. Theirs was a religion without mercy, without kindness and lacking in grace. A religion about power and prestige, not love and brokenness.

The tax collector stood apart, not to make a statement of his own righteousness but because he didn't feel worthy to stand with God's people before the altar. His prayer and his actions broke any stereotype that could be made of him. The Pharisee publicly renounced the tax collector, but he made the grave mistake which we humans so easily fall into—the mistake of judging from the outside.

There were several postures of prayer for a Jew, one of which, for contrition, was eyes down and hands across the chest, but this man broke tradition and began to beat on his chest. It was a gesture most often used by women in times of intense anger or anguish; for men it was a gesture seldom used. It occurs only one other place in the New Testament, in Luke 23:46–48:

> Jesus called out with a loud voice, 'Father, into your hands I commit my spirit.' When he had said this, he breathed his last.
>
> The centurion, seeing what had happened, praised God and said, 'Surely this was a righteous man.' When all the people who had gathered to witness this sight saw what took place, they beat their breasts and went away. But all those who knew him, including the women who had followed him from Galilee, stood at a distance, watching these things.

It took the magnitude of Golgotha to elicit this response. It was a sign of deep remorse, and the tax collector used it as a symbol of his longing to stand with the righteous. His prayer was not general but specific, yearning for mercy, aware that he needed help to be made right with God.

Self-righteousness distorts vision. The Pharisee only saw a sinner to be avoided.

The world is repelled by cold and judgemental forms of religion. It is much easier to be a Pharisee than it is to follow Jesus, because to follow Jesus means to look at the world without prejudice or bias.

The tax collectors and sinners gathered around

Jesus because he was accessible, warm and friendly. It's difficult for even the most hardened heart to resist unconditional love. Jesus was different, and he calls us to be different as well. Not in a weird religious way, but in the way we deal with brokenness. Pharisaism has never been on the cutting edge of God's grace and power because it emphasises righteousness by works.

4

The Difference That Love Makes

There are no victories in all of our histories without love (Sting).

God's people have always battled with exclusivity. It was never God's intention to separate his people for any other purpose than to make them an army by which his kingdom could be manifested on the earth. In the Old Testament book of Jonah, the Children of Israel were reminded by God of their priorities. Jonah the prophet could see no worth in the Ninevites. He saw only a people worthy of judgement, but God saw a people in need of redemption. The darkness that permeated the lives of the people of Nineveh is a reminder of what the world is like without God's love.

After a battle with his own soul, Jonah finally obeyed God and went to Nineveh to prophesy against it. In his heart, he expected God to destroy the city. Again, his perspective was wrong, as the people of Nineveh responded to the message of judgement with repentance. This really made Jonah angry and God had to challenge Jonah's perspectives once again. Jonah was happy to receive God's blessing in his own life, but considered others

unworthy of the same. God's heart, however, is for
redemption, and he constantly looks for people to
stand in the gap and seek mercy for a fallen world.

The world without God's love at work in it is not a
pretty place. One glance at the television news, with
its constant diet of man's inhumanity to man,
violence, injustice and hate, reminds us that people
who live without God's love don't make the world a
better place. Our history labours on the achievements of man. As someone once said, 'History is
always written by the winners.'

Our perspective as human beings is on all the
great things that we humans have accomplished—
our advances in science, literature, medicine, etc.
But an honest investigation of human history
reveals not only the achievements of mankind, but
also the incredible darkness woven throughout our
story. As you look back over the course of human
history, what stands out are not the high achievements, but rather century after century of man's
violence to man. The Roman empire, world wars,
the incredible list of butchers who pepper the scenario; Stalin, Hitler, Pinochet, Caucescu, to name
but a few in our generation alone. Along with the
global sweep of national and international violence,
we also discover in our own society the continuing
issues of rising crimes, domestic violence, child
abuse and all the other issues that paint the picture
of what the world is like without God's love.

Our world has a terrible concept of love. The
entertainment media proffer many ideas about love.

On one occasion Jesus was invited to the home of
a Pharisee. It was common practice in those days to
invite young teachers after meetings in the synagogue to dine with the other leaders to discuss

theology, etc. The intention of this particular man was not to build a relationship with Jesus but basically to insult him and to seek to discredit his ministry. All of the traditional acts of welcome were ignored and Jesus was insulted. It was like being invited to someone's house for dinner and then being left in the hallway with your hat and coat on while your host dined.

In Jesus' time dinners were an open affair and people could walk past and watch the proceedings. On this occasion, a woman was present who had lived a sordid past. Seeing the breach of etiquette and the intentional insults directed at Jesus, she was moved to perform a unique act to defend Jesus' honour. The Pharisee, of course, was horrified. A prostitute had invaded his home and jeopardised the purity of his household. Not only that, she was making a public spectacle of herself and validating the opinion already formed by the Pharisee about Jesus. She had come sweeping into the room and fallen at Jesus' feet crying. With her tears she washed Jesus' feet, and then with her hair she wiped them dry.

It was a horrible sin for a woman to let her hair down in public, but she did not stop there. She began to kiss his feet and then she poured perfume on them. It was common for prostitutes to wear a jar of perfume around their neck in Jesus' day. It was a sign of their profession, and they would anoint themselves in order to smell good for their clients.

There was incredible symbolism in her actions. There were many forms of greeting used to denote relationship in Jewish culture. To kiss someone's feet was to acknowledge their role as a noble person. The Pharisee's action was to imply that Jesus was of an inferior rank, but the woman's action reversed that. More than a compensation for the insult hurled at Jesus, it was also a public gesture of humility and devotion.

When the Pharisee witnessed this, he made some remarks to himself: 'If this man were a prophet he would know who is touching him and what kind of woman she is—that she is a sinner.' Once again he revealed the common preconceptions about holiness and religious posture: that the basic requirement of right relationship with God is one of distance and removal from anything or anyone deemed unclean. In fact, this Pharisee was so blinded by his religion that he could not see a human being but simply a sinner; someone to be avoided at all costs. But things change, and so can people when 'love comes to town'.

That this woman had lived a sinful life was not in question, but something had changed. By the nature of her profession, she was accustomed to dealing with and handling men, but there was something different about this Jesus. Here was a man, loving to women, giving them respect and dignity. A man with whom one could be close and yet safe. She had never met a man like this before and her encounter with Jesus changed her life. She had been a prostitute, but that was before she met Jesus. Her actions in washing his feet with her tears and drying them with her hair were spontaneous responses to the situation before her, but there is reason to believe that she came to the dinner intent on anointing Jesus' feet with the tool of her trade. First to signify her devotion to Jesus, but also to signal the end of one portion of her life and the start of another. She poured out the tool of her trade on Jesus' feet, symbolising the end of her sinful ways.

Amazingly, the Pharisee was unable to see in any of these actions the change that had taken place in her life. His bias kept her locked in her past, but she was a different woman now. Wherever Jesus walked, he effected change. He was willing to walk where no other religious leader had ever walked, and everywhere he went, he brought not a self-righteous judgementalism that characterised the religious leaders of his day, but the all-inclusive love of God available to every man.

5

Love's Response to Sin

The way in which Jesus dealt with the issue of sin was also remarkable. He never allowed an individual's sin to get in the way of his love. When a woman was brought before him, having been caught in the act of adultery, a great challenge was placed before Jesus. The intent of those who brought the woman was to seek to undermine Jesus' ministry and build a case against him. It was well known by everybody that the law demanded swift and immediate judgement: death by stoning. There seemed to be no escape for Jesus. His tenderness towards the fallen was a great irritation to the religious leaders, but here it seemed as though they had him. This was no vague accusation of adultery. The woman had literally been caught in the act and hauled publicly before Jesus, who was teaching in the temple. Any Jew with the scantest knowledge of the law of Moses knew the command, and there seemed to be no way to reinterpret and find a way of escape.

One of the accounts records that Jesus did not answer for a time and when he did, his reply astonished all present: 'If any one of you is without sin, let him be the first to throw a stone at her' (Jn 8:7b). This statement was not a watering down of the law but its true interpretation. The law was not given to enable men to use it as a hammer with which to hit each other; it was given as a reminder that no man can stand upright before God except by God's grace and mercy.

Needless to say, Jesus' answer to their question thinned the crowd and eventually all the accusers disappeared until Jesus was left with the humiliated woman. His response to her captures the heart of the ministry of Jesus: 'Woman, where are they? Has no-one condemned you?'

'No-one sir,' she said.

'Then neither do I condemn you,' Jesus declared. 'Go now and leave your life of sin.'

His love for the woman was not compromised by her sinful acts, but neither was his stand against sin compromised by his love. It was that unique ability to stand for righteousness and holiness while maintaining an incredible love for fallen mankind which made Jesus the compelling religious leader that he was. Jesus was far less concerned about what people had done in the past than he was about making certain that they had found forgiveness and were walking on the new path. He wanted to confirm forgiveness, not highlight her sinfulness.

The law was not given to provide ammunition with which to attack people who obviously failed in observing that law. It was given as a tool by which people could be made whole. The effectiveness of Jesus' ministry, and any ministry done in his name, is shaped by an awareness of the brokenness of human life and a desire to see it whole.

6

The Ministry That Makes a Difference

It has hands to help others, it has feet to hurry to the poor and needy—it has eyes to see the misery and want. It has ears to hear the sighs and sorrows of mankind. This is what love looks like (Augustine).[8]

The church must be ready to speak the truth in love. It has a responsibility for all, the rich and the poor, the ruler and the ruled, the oppressed and the oppressor, but it needs to point out that God does take sides. Incredibly, He sides with those whom the world would marginalise, whom the world considers of little account. That was what He did in the founding of Israel. He took their side when they did not deserve it against the powerful; against Pharaoh. That was a paradigmatic act that gave an important clue about the sort of God He is (Desmond Tutu).[9]

When John the Baptist was imprisoned and wondering about Jesus, he sent his followers to seek Jesus out and ask him a question. 'Are you the Messiah or should we be looking for someone else?' they asked. Jesus' reply not only answered their question about his Messiahship, but also gave shape to his ministry and its purpose. 'Go back and report to John what you hear and see: The blind receive sight, the lame walk, those who have leprosy are cured, the deaf hear, the dead are raised, and the good news is preached to the poor' (Mt 11:4–5).

The essence of Jesus' ministry was given to John. Jesus came to the outcast of this world, those marginalised by society, the ones overlooked and discounted, and made them central to the purposes of God. Jesus came to validate the fact that every human life is valuable and precious in the sight of God. There was a throwaway attitude towards the insignificant in Jesus' day, as there is today. But Jesus demonstrated the reality of David's statement in the Psalms that we are 'fearfully and wonderfully made' (Ps 139:14).

The great champion of the poor, Lord Shaftesbury, was once asked in the Houses of Parliament, 'Why do you concern yourself about these people, these common people?' Shaftesbury replied, 'I am concerned about these people because they, like us, are created by the same God, redeemed by the same Saviour, and destined for the same immortality.'[10]

Jesus cared for the unlovely because God cares for them. Jesus also said that the poor would always be with us and the great challenge for us as followers of Jesus is how we will deal with them.

Jesus did not look at people simply as objects to practise ministry on. You can learn a lot about people from their attitudes and responses towards the unlovable and the unlovely. It's quite easy to embrace people who at least by outward appearances seem acceptable. Fringe people tend to make us nervous; those outside of our comfort zones can bring out the worst in us. We respond with everything from nervous laughter to patronisation and even scorn. The innocence of children is often marred by the playground taunts which they direct at those who don't fit in for some reason—perhaps due to a physical or emotional deformity. But Jesus embraced the lepers in a society which regarded the leper as many regard the AIDS victim today. Jesus broke with convention and did something they never experienced before. Through him they felt the touch of a human being untouched by their disease—not one who was in the same predicament, but one who saw their predicament and cared for them.

We will probably never understand the humiliation of being outcast because of something that has happened to us. Leprosy was a disease so feared that not only were lepers cast out of towns and villages, but whenever they came close to civilisation they had to announce their uncleanness so that they could be avoided. We will never grasp the impact that the touch of Jesus must have made upon them. He cleansed the demonised and dined with publicans and prostitutes. He truly cared about the unwanted and in no uncertain terms made those whose attitude was different understand that he saw his role in life as an ambassador to the unwanted; that he came for the sick and the blind, and not for those who claimed to be healthy and have sight.

As he walked through the streets of London in the latter part of the last century, William Booth, founder of the Salvation Army, saw the incredible despair of the poor in their slums. He found among the drunk, the purposeless, the thieves and the pickpockets, a people who needed to know the love of God. Those people who had been overlooked, ignored and rejected were to become the focus of his life. William Booth had tapped into that unique ability that Jesus had: to see people with the eyes of eternity; to see beyond what they were, to what they were meant to be.

> As Jesus went on from there, he saw a man named Matthew sitting at the tax collector's booth. 'Follow me,' he told him, and Matthew got up and followed him.
>
> While Jesus was having dinner at Matthew's house, many tax collectors and 'sinners' came and ate with him and his disciples. When the Pharisees saw this, they asked his disciples, 'Why does your teacher eat with tax collectors and "sinners"?'
>
> On hearing this, Jesus said, 'It is not the healthy who need a doctor, but the sick. But go and learn what this means: "I desire mercy, not sacrifice." For I have not come to call the righteous, but sinners' (Mt 9:9–13).

The men whom Jesus chose to be his closest followers didn't appear too promising from the outside, but he saw something in them that no one else could see. He knew that lives could be transformed and the worst of human beings could become the best. As we read through the Gospels we see flashes of brilliance in the lives of the twelve, but more often than not we find Peter with his foot in his mouth and James and John calling down fire on unsuspecting villages! There is no record of any of them being well educated or well positioned socially, and yet to these men Jesus committed the future of his kingdom, without a reserve team just in case they should fail. The world still marginalises people; people who don't fit the mould, who don't seem to possess all of the abilities it takes to make it in the world. Jesus was not content to see people as they were, but as they could become. He saw the 'rock' in

Peter, the honesty in Matthew, a corrupt tax collector, and the opportunity that every man could have to be changed by the presence of his kingdom.

> Woe to you, teachers of the law and Pharisees, you hypocrites! You give a tenth of your spices—mint, dill and cummin. But you have neglected the more important matters of the law—justice, mercy and faithfulness. You should have practised the latter, without neglecting the former. You blind guides! You strain out a gnat but swallow a camel (Mt 23:23–24).

No religious leader has had as much effect on modern thought as Jesus has. He stands in a place by himself because of the many different priorities by which he lived. In contrast to the bulk of the religious teachers and thinkers from all streams, Jesus stands out in regard to his view and his thinking in relationship to the human body. The interest he showed in physical and mental healing is remarkably materialistic for the world of the spirit. A large portion of the Gospels are records of his healing ministry. He not only proclaimed and taught the good news of the kingdom, but demonstrated with power the life of the kingdom. During his ministry on earth, he sent his disciples out, not only to announce his kingdom, but also to share in his healing ministry.

According to many scholars, Jesus had a unique view of man—quite different from the main view of his time. In his day a common view was that every individual was in control of himself, able to determine actions by his own conscious choice. If a man had knowledge of right and wrong, he would do the right thing. Evil deeds were regarded as the result of ill-will. Jesus did not dispute that. In fact one of the marks of Christian thinking should be a developed sense of right and wrong. But Jesus also saw man as dominated by forces beyond his control and that man at times was powerless to triumph over those forces: 'As he went along, he saw a man blind from birth. His disciples asked him, "Rabbi, who sinned, this man or his parents, that he was born blind?" "Neither this man nor his parents sinned," said Jesus, "but this happened so that the work of God might be displayed in his life"' (Jn 9:1–3).

When it came to sickness and sin, Jesus was antagonistic. There is a sense in the Gospels that Jesus was pained by people bound up in infirmity, and in compassion, the power of God was poured out on the needy. In Jesus' day, as quite often in ours, there was an underlying sense that sickness was always the result of sin and one of God's punishments. In the thirteenth-century church a man had to confess to a priest before a doctor would visit. Jesus never portrayed sin as a total cause of sickness, and even when there was reference to the role of sin, Jesus still took action to bring healing, manifesting understanding and compassion rather than judgement.

It is quite remarkable how often in his earthly ministry Jesus took time to heal insignificant people—such as Bartimaeus whom everyone else tried to keep quiet. Jesus, however, made time for him. What made the healing of Bartimaeus all the more revealing about Jesus' priorities is that it took place shortly after Jesus had predicted his death to the disciples and while, in fact, he was on his way to Jerusalem to face the horror of the cross. He rebuked the demons and demonic powers that bound and crippled people and he claimed healing to be a good work, telling the Pharisees that they regarded the saving of an animal which had fallen into a pit on the Sabbath as valuable enough to break the laws of the Sabbath. Six times there are recorded healings performed by Jesus on the Sabbath, showing that whenever there was opportunity to help the infirm that it was a good thing and important enough that rituals ought not to stand in the way.

7

Words That Made the Difference

No-one ever spoke the way this man does (Jn 7:46).

It takes two to speak the truth—one to speak and another to hear (Henry David Thoreau).

Studying in the solitude of the mountains is not equal to sitting at the crossroads and listening to the talk of men (S. G. Champion).

Jesus used religious language uniquely. He spoke in ways which ordinary people understood. He had the ability to take abstract concepts dealing with the issues of God and his kingdom and communicate them in such a way that everyone could hear. In fact, so compelling were his teachings that people flocked by the thousands to wherever he was and put off going home until the last possible moment. The people of the Bible were human beings just like you and I, governed pretty much by their stomachs, and yet on at least one occasion the crowds were so enthralled by Jesus' stories that even dinner was put on hold.

Jesus took the common everyday instances of life and used them to paint pictures of the kingdom. His stories were captivating and colourful. He knew how to penetrate people's vulnerability. They let their

53

defences down when they were around him and he
could then speak into their condition. It has been
said that people often have to hear, but they don't
have to listen. In order to make people listen, their
attention must be captured. The graphic stories that
Jesus used tell us a lot about the kind of person he
was. It is quite obvious that he was no ivory tower
theologian using the language of the ancients to
convey lofty and obscure theological concepts and
truths. The teachings of Jesus were powerful, captivating and earthy.

One of the great truths of the Bible is that God
became flesh and dwelt among us. Jesus became
more than just human. He became a man who lived
a real life in a real world and was familiar with the
harsh reality and grim routine of human existence.
He put that knowledge and understanding to great
use. There was amazement at the teachings of Jesus,
not simply because of the outrageous things he said,
but because he spoke in the language of the
common man. The realities of the kingdom of
heaven are things that you can't draw. They are
obscure concepts like justification, sanctification,
redemption and holiness. These great truths are
vital to grasp, but they are quite often beyond most
people's understanding. Jesus used things which
people understood—farming, growing, animals—
everyday situations to illustrate the principles of the
kingdom of God.

He used riches and the discovery of hidden treasure to convey the value and the joy that comes to
those who discover the kingdom. In Jewish life, it
was quite common to hide valuables in the ground
to protect them, and sometimes one could come
across a treasure trove. What man if he found such a

treasure wouldn't rush home to sell everything in order to buy the land where the treasure was hidden? You can almost hear the sounds of agreement and see people identifying with the story and thinking out loud how lucky that man would be. Having captured their attention with a story they could all relate to, Jesus then related the story to the kingdom and told the gathered listeners that the kingdom of heaven was more priceless than any treasure, and worth the sacrifice of everything else in order to obtain it.

We can glimpse humour in the stories of Jesus. A camel through the eye of a needle? Some scholars have tried to theologise the meaning and say it refers to some hidden gate in the temple that camels could squeeze through. The bottom line, however, is quite simply that Jesus was using exaggerated extremes to convey deep truth. The people stayed because his words were compelling and entertaining. He is the example that biblical truth does not have to be cold and clinical.

The Apostle Paul also realised the need to communicate heavenly truth in a relevant way. When he was in Athens, a city given to any and every new idea, he used poetry from one of their own philosophers to lay the foundation for his presentation of the gospel (Acts 17). The world around us presents a rich field of creative images for presenting the gospel.

'Life-changing preaching does not talk to the people about the Bible. Instead, it talks to the people about themselves—their questions, hurts, fears, and struggles—from the Bible' (Haddon Robinson).[11]

It has always been interesting to me that in Acts 2, when the Holy Spirit fell on the group assembled in the Upper Room, they began to speak forth the gospel in such a way that every man heard it in his own language. God could have made everyone hear it in perfect biblical Hebrew, but he chose to speak to them in their common languages. Even the Cretans heard the gospel in their language, and they were a very motley crew. Paul said, 'Even one of their own prophets has said, "Cretans are always liars, evil brutes, lazy gluttons." This testimony is true' (Tit 1:12–13).

God is always interested in communicating with anyone willing to listen. Jesus made listening so much more enjoyable because his words were accessible and his stories real.

8

Love That Breaks the Rules

The heart of the Christian Gospel is precisely that God the holy One, the all powerful One, is also the One full of mercy and compassion. He is not a neutral God inhabiting some inaccessible Mount of Olympus. He is a God who cares about his children and cares enormously for the weak, the poor, the naked, the downtrodden, the despised. He takes their side not because they are good, since many of them are demonstrably not so. He takes their side because He is that kind of God, and they have no one else to champion them (Desmond Tutu).[12]

If you are going to kick authority in the teeth—you might as well use two feet (Keith Richards).[13]

Sometimes you've just gotta break the rules (Burger King slogan).

Do not think that I have come to abolish the Law or the Prophets; I have not come to abolish them but to fulfil them. I tell you the truth, until heaven and earth disappear, not the smallest letter, not the least stroke of a pen, will by any means disappear from the Law until everything is accomplished (Mt 5:17–18).

Jesus continually broke traditions and challenged the interpretations of the religionists, but he was never anti-establishment just for the sake of it. He simply lived by the maxim: people before the law. When God gave the law to the children of Israel, it was for the good of people and society. It was never the desire of God to squeeze the joy out of life, lest we forget he is the Creator and he spared nothing to give us a world pleasing to the eye and joyful to the heart.

However, the law was placed in the hands of men who, over the course of time, scrutinised, examined, considered and explained its meaning over and over again. Eventually, with the deep insight of men, additions were made, until in Jesus' day there were 613 laws to observe, 248 of which were called 'weighty', and 365 called 'light'. When the 'light' laws were violated this was treated more leniently. Laws with regard to the Sabbath were held most sacred and it was these laws, and the keeping or breaking of them, which brought about most confrontation between Jesus and the religious orthodoxy.

A prime example is found in John 5. It is a simple little story of Jesus healing a man who had been an invalid for thirty-eight years. The story would probably have simply been another account of Jesus' miracle ministry were it not for the words recorded in verses 9–10: 'The day on which this took place was a Sabbath, and so the Jews said to the man who had been healed, "It is the Sabbath, the law forbids you to carry your mat"'!

To them it was much better for the man to stay an invalid than to be healed on their holy day and violate the law by carrying what had once been his sick bed. They didn't respond with joy to the healing, or consider that after lying down by a pool every day for thirty-eight years, carrying his mat was not work (which was illegal on the Sabbath), but

more a celebration of God's mercy. Neither did they
take time to consider the messianic implications of
what had taken place. They only saw violations.
Rules were rules and could never be broken.

It didn't occur to them to consider the incredible
events taking place in their life and times. It wasn't
every day that someone showed up in Jerusalem
with the ability to heal. You can understand why
Jesus wept over the city and for a people ignorant of
what was taking place among them. Here were a
people living for the advent of their Messiah. That
was their blessed hope. But he walked among them
and they knew it not. The religious leaders of Israel
were not happy that a man had been set free; they
were outraged. They didn't want a man to receive
God's mercy on a holy day. They did not see the
evidence of Jesus' ministry, only his 'radicalness'. He
simply refused to fit into their mould. They were
encrusted by rules and regulations, and human
need was no longer a consideration. Jesus showed
the difference between using and abusing rules and
he made the definitive statement, that the emphasis
of the kingdom of heaven is compassion, love and
faithfulness to God and to others, not outward
behaviour. Jesus broke with tradition and crossed
barriers, generally because some form of prejudice
stood in the way of someone's need.

'You have heard it said, but I say unto you . . .'
Jesus frequently declared in the Gospels. He came
not to overthrow the law but to reinterpret it to a
world gone wrong. In our culture we understand
good guy/bad guy roles so we can detect the gist of
many of Jesus' stories. But never did Jesus so
blatantly cross barriers as when he brought up the
issues of women and Samaritans.

The Jews would not speak civilly of a Samaritan because the racial tension and hatred ran so deep. The problem went back hundreds of years to a time when the Samaritan Jews had intermarried and so defiled their heritage. Over the course of time, this betrayal became a source of division and ultimately of rival worship as the Samaritans—rejected by what were technically their fellow Jews—built their own temple on Mount Gerizim.

> He that eats the bread of the Samaritans is liked to one that eats the flesh of swine (Mishna Shebiith 8:10, Danby 49).[14]

Even an unrighteous Jew would not associate with a Samaritan. They were to be avoided at all costs. Understanding that tension, it is enlightening to see how often Jesus used Samaritans in his stories as heroes. This was unthinkable.

Perhaps nowhere was Jesus' use of a Samaritan hero as cutting as in the story of the Good Samaritan. Here Jesus confronted bigotry and bias head on. In his story, he told not of a Jew overcoming his prejudice and reaching out to a wounded Samaritan, but of a Samaritan reaching across the barriers erected against him to help someone, who would certainly have rejected his help if he were conscious. The road from Jerusalem to Jericho was notoriously dangerous: a steep vulnerable seventeen-mile journey from about 3,000 feet above sea level to 1,000 feet below sea level. It was nicknamed 'the Bloody Way' and yet, in spite of the danger, it was the primary means of getting from one place to another.

Jesus told the story of a man being attacked, robbed and left naked and unconscious. Without clothes and unable to communicate, the man had no means by which to identify himself. In the story (Lk 10:25–37), the first man to arrive on the scene was a priest on his way from Jerusalem down to Jericho. Historians have noted that many of the priests who served in the temple lived in Jericho and would journey up to Jerusalem for their two weeks of service. The implication is that he was on his way home. There are many factors that come into play in this story. For a priest to serve in the temple he had to be 'clean'. There were many laws about purity and cleanness. For example, a priest should not associate with foreigners and should not come within a certain distance of a dead man. As Jesus told the story, the priest encountered the body and passed by on the other side of the road. How did he know if the man was alive? If he had investigated and found the man to be dead or a foreigner, he would have been 'unclean' and required to return to Jerusalem for a week of very costly ritual cleansing.

The man journeyed on only to be followed a short while later by a Levite, also someone involved in the temple worship services. His response was much the same as the priest's and the man remained in the road, naked and wounded.

There were three groups of people who served in the temple: priests, Levites and lay people. Up to this point Jesus' story was following a predictable path, but then Jesus introduced a horrifying twist. Suddenly a Samaritan appeared. To the listening audience this would have raised every nationalistic, racist and bigoted attitude. Once again, Jesus reversed the stereotype and in the light of the actions of the two preceding men, who were religious men and accustomed to handling the law, the Samaritan put his life at risk and went to the aid of a man he was unable to identify. Not only did the Samaritan help the man in his immediate crisis, he then proceeded to lay aside his own schedule and took the time to get the man to help. He then spent the night with him. Then, in the morning, he not only left extra money for the man's recuperation but he also committed himself to assuming any added debt. Jesus showed the Samaritan crossing boundaries and reaching out in a true expression of worship to God.

Jesus told the story to confront a barrier that the religious people had erected. It came in response to a question Jesus had been asked: 'Who is my neighbour?' (Lk 10:29). The person who had asked the question had done so to test Jesus to see if he would undermine the law, which was regarded as the means by which the Jews would inherit eternal life. But once again the 'experts' had turned Scripture inside out as they sought to find the limits; the least that one could get away with doing. In telling the story of the Good Samaritan, Jesus reinterpreted the question to ask not, 'Who is my neighbour?' but rather, 'To whom do I act neighbourly?'. The first question seeks limits; the second leaves room for the unconditional love and mercy of God. We must never ask, 'Who should I love?' but, 'Do I love without discrimination, reservation or hesitation?'

Another area where Jesus crossed barriers was with regard to women. Jewish society was patriarchal and male dominated. Women were regarded as little more than chattel and definitely as second-class citizens. Jesus, however, saw them very differently. The fact that Jesus called twelve male disciples could easily leave us with the impression that Jesus' entourage was exclusively a male bastion. But if we look beyond that, it is quite obvious that a number of women played a significant role in his life. In an age when education was reserved for males Jesus taught women. When the Bible records the feeding of the five thousand men, it also tells us that women were present, not only for the food, but also for the teaching. That was an amazing statement of women's rights and a validation of their capacity to learn and understand. This was not recognised by their culture.

Jesus taught the Samaritan woman at the well about reality of life and worship. Cultural tension, religious bias and the dominant male-centred lifestyle should have precluded that conversation ever taking place. He spent a great deal of time with Mary and Martha at Bethany. One of Jesus' most insightful teachings on priority and perspective was directed at these two women. Rather than simply allowing them to cater to his every need and serve him, he saw once again the necessity of reaching out and educating both the ladies.

Not only did Jesus affirm women's ability to understand and learn by freely and openly teaching them along with the men, he also affirmed their spiritual capabilities. Among the Jews of that time, the issue of women's salvation was suspect. There was a horrible chauvinism that pervaded this society built on patriarchs which reduced women to mere flesh-and-blood beings.

In Luke 8 Jesus was asked by a religious ruler to go and minister to his twelve-year-old daughter, who was dying. As Jesus attempted to make his way to the man's house, the crowds almost crushed him. In the midst of that crowd was a woman with a humiliating and socially unacceptable female problem. She pressed through the crowd to touch the edge of Jesus' cloak, and immediately, after twelve years of illness, was healed. '"Who touched me?" Jesus asked' (Lk 8:45). Everyone denied touching him, and Peter said they were all touching him! But Jesus had come to confront a world of brokenness and sin, and that is never achieved without cost. 'Power has gone out from me,' were his words. He knew the difference between the press of the crowd and the touch of someone dead seeking life. It turned out to be a woman and she came fearfully and fell at his feet. She began to tell Jesus in front of all the people why she had touched him and how she'd been healed. 'Daughter, your faith has healed you . . .' In front of the assembled crowd Jesus affirmed her capacity. She could see in him what many of the most religious were unable to.

Then there was Jesus' encounter with the Canaanite woman. She found deliverance through her persistence, humility and insight. If ever there was an incident where Jesus seemed hostile to women, it would have been this one. She came to Jesus seeking help for her daughter and Jesus made every effort to turn her away. He claimed that his ministry was exclusively towards the Israelites, and yet she still persisted. 'It is not right to take the children's bread and toss it to their dogs.' Not exactly a pleasant rebuttal. Her answer drew affirmation and answer from Jesus. 'Yes Lord, but even the dogs eat the crumbs that fall from their master's table.' Then Jesus answered, 'Woman, you have great faith! Your request is granted.' She acknowledged her position as a dog—one outside the blessing of the kingdom—but once again she had insight into the person of Jesus, and her spiritual capacity was validated.

Every time Jesus talked to women, it was done with respect and dignity. Many of our Bibles translate his address to women as 'Woman . . .' which in our culture is not the politest form of addressing females. But in Jesus' day it was definitely more of an acknowledgement of the beauty of womanhood than a condescending response. It was the term with which he addressed his mother from the cross as he presented her with a new son, and it was also the term with which he addressed the woman caught in adultery. In both cases the sense of his address is one of care, compassion and respect.

Jesus used women in his stories in much the same way as Samaritans, in order to portray the issues of the kingdom. It was a woman who was used as a model for the way in which we should seek the kingdom when she showed tenacity, perseverance and commitment in sweeping the house to find a lost coin. It was the widow's sacrificial giving and the widow's persevering prayer that were examples for us all. In a world of male dominance and arrogance Jesus again broke the rules in order to communicate the value God places on all human life.

9

Love and Forgiveness

I've been trying to get down to the heart of the matter . . . I think it's about forgiveness (Don Henley, Mike Campbell, J. D. Souther).[15]

Father, forgive them, for they do not know what they are doing (Lk 23:34).

Men will probably debate until the end of time as to which were the greatest words ever spoken by a man. There will be advocates for the lyrical poetry of Shakespeare. There will be those who will put forth the great sayings of Buddha and Confuscius, the passionate writings of Tolstoy, and the heart-moving speeches of men like Churchill, Lincoln, Ghandi and Martin Luther King Jr. But surely no words can carry more power, more beauty and more love than the words uttered by Jesus as he hung dying on the cross, a sacrifice for all mankind. In the midst of horrific pain and the agonising torture of crucifixion, surrounded by a hostile, mocking and jeering crowd, those words 'Father, forgive . . .' hang as an indictment over all mankind and prove that surely there is a dereliction and blindness fundamental to human experience and behaviour.

66

It wasn't solely at the end of his life that Christ manifested forgiveness. His earthly ministry, his constant extending of forgiveness, was a source of tension between him and his protagonists. 'When Jesus saw their faith, he said [to the paralytic], "Friend, your sins are forgiven." The Pharisees and the teachers of the law began thinking to themselves, "Who is this fellow who speaks blasphemy? Who can forgive sins but God alone?"' (Lk 5:20–21).

Jesus came to announce God's judgement on a guilty world, but the sentence was a surprise: forgiveness and mercy. Jesus taught his disciples that the heart of the kingdom was love, and that from that love forgiveness should spring forth. Men prefer vindication or revenge but Jesus challenged that and everywhere he went he released the forgiveness of God.

Peter came to Jesus seeking where the limit to forgiveness lay. Being generous, he said, 'How many times shall I forgive my brother who sins against me? Seven times?' Interestingly enough, there is a story in the Old Testament of a man by the name of Lamech. He was a man who sought revenge for wrong done to himself, and he made this declaration: 'Adah and Zillah, listen to me; wives of Lamech, hear my words. I have killed a man for wounding me, a young man for injuring me. If Cain is avenged seven times, then Lamech seventy-seven times' (Gen 4:23–24).

Lamech spoke of unlimited revenge, and perhaps in reference to that, Jesus responded to Peter with the challenge to unlimited forgiveness. Jesus' world, like ours, was full of the tensions of human relationships—everything from family disputes to

national and international tensions. To that world
he brought forgiveness, and challenges his followers
to do the same. The essence of the kingdom is that
since we have been forgiven, we should forgive.
When he taught the disciples to pray, the issue of
forgiveness was at the heart of the prayer, the
principle and the reminder being that as recipients
of undeserved mercy and forgiveness, it is
imperative that we mete out the same. The parable
of the unjust steward is a chilling reminder of what
happens when those who have been forgiven take
for granted that gift.

Debt was a major problem in first-century
Palestine, as it is today, although the reasons for it
are probably not the same. Debt was the bane of
Jesus' society, not because of excessive consumer
credit, but because the poor continually sought to
stave off hardship and ruin with visits to the money
lenders. You may remember the story in Matthew
18 of a man called to settle his indebtedness only to
discover his inability to repay. His debt was enor-
mous. Not the ordinary debt of a man whose crop
had failed, but one that would take lifetimes to
repay. The king to whom he owed the money
responded in an extraordinary manner and wiped
away the debt at great cost to himself. Immediately
afterwards, the man, now freed from any obligation,
encountered someone who owed him a pittance in
comparison and yet his treatment of him was brutal.
Jesus told this story to convey that the starting
point of everything is the immense and undeserved
love and forgiveness of God. Secondly, the only
proper response to that is love for others. Disciples
of Jesus are called not simply to love their neighbour
in ways in which they would like to be treated, but in

the way that they themselves have been treated by God.

Those haunting words from the cross challenge us today as they did when Christ walked the earth. 'Father forgive them, for they do not know what they are doing.'

10

Love That Gives Itself Away

Love, soft as an easy chair ('Evergreen').

Then he said to them all: 'If anyone would come after me, he must deny himself and take up his cross daily and follow me' (Lk 9:23).

The Bible says in Hebrews that Jesus, for the joy that was set before him, endured the cross, despising the shame. It was obedience that led Jesus to the cross. Obedience always conjures up negative conotations in my mind: something that one must do because the person asking is bigger. Yet obedience in the life of Jesus was something quite different. Jesus lived his life in complete obedience to the Father. 'The Son can do nothing by himself; he can do only what he sees his Father doing, because whatever the Father does the Son also does. For the Father loves the Son and shows him all he does' (Jn 5:19–20).

This was the principle by which Jesus lived. We could say that Jesus had a life that was planless and yet not aimless. His goal was simply to do all that the Father asked of him. He was obedient to God even as the cost of obedience rose towards the end of his life. In the Garden of Gethsemane at the most crucial point of his life, and the most precarious for us, Jesus chose to do that which would display the wonder of the Father's love to us.

As human beings, we generally tend to stumble when it comes to making choices and following paths that are perhaps more beneficial to others than to ourselves. Jesus gave his disciples one of the foundational principles upon which his kingdom was built at a very strategic moment in his earthly ministry. He had commissioned and empowered the disciples to go out and preach the kingdom of God. He had fed 5,000 men and their families, and when it was over he went to pray with his disciples. In that moment of quietness, Jesus asked his friends an important question: 'Who do the crowds say that I am?' They replied with the words from the streets about who they thought Jesus was. It was an interesting collection of ideas.

Some thought that Jesus was John the Baptist, and in many ways there was a similarity between the two of them, neither one was a theorist but more a practical exponent of walking with God on a daily basis. Both their ministries were characterised by the call to repentance.

Other people thought that maybe Jesus was Elijah, the prophet of the prophets. In Jewish culture it was said that Elijah would return at the end of the ages, and in Jesus' time with Roman oppressors and Jewish zealots, there was a sense of climax and hunger among the people for power. Jesus' ministry was also characterised by power, unseen among the plethora of religious teachers.

Most of the people weren't too sure who Jesus was at all. They had a sense that perhaps he was a prophet. His ministry was too powerful to be ignored, and they figured that if nothing else he must have been any one of the prophets of old come back to life.

Once Jesus had gleaned the opinion of the masses about him, he then directed the same question to his closest friends: those who had experienced everything with him. Peter answered for them all: 'You are the Christ, the Son of the living God.' Jesus told them not to tell anyone, and then proceeded to speak of his rejection and death. Hardly the words of a triumphant Messiah. The disciples weren't sure what to think of all this. I'm sure that it was hardly the response they were expecting. But there was in the midst of all this one area of promise. He spoke of building a church upon this revelation. A people of victory over the prevailing weaknesses of prejudice and self-centredness in our world—a people against whom the very gates of hell would have no success. He spoke of building a people of power out of those who found their life and identity in him. He then gave them the key, not only to his life, but also to the means by which they could become the people of power. He called them to deny themselves, take up their cross and follow him. It hardly seemed to be the stuff that powerful kingdoms are built upon. And yet, that was the source of Jesus' power: giving himself away, willingly bowing to the desires of the Father, moving to act in love towards others. That was the cornerstone by which he would build a people. The church against which the powers of hell cannot triumph is the church giving itself away in the Father's name to a world destroyed by self-ishness. Jesus' life and ministry were marked by this unique characteristic of selflessness. Nowhere was this more greatly demonstrated than in the Garden of Gethsemane, when he arose from prayer fully prepared for the agony of the cross, and set out with joy to his destiny.

Obedience to Jesus was not a heavy load to bear. He came to show man what it was like to walk with God, and he wore obedience not as a shackle, but as a joyous privilege given to men. There is a power in obedience not recognised by our world, but a man fully yielded to God turned water to wine, opened blind eyes and fed to the multitudes the bread of life.

11

You've Got to Pray

You got to pray just to make it through the day (MC Hammer, 'Pray').

But when you pray, do not be like the hypocrites, for they love to pray standing in the synagogues and on the street corners to be seen by men. I tell you the truth, they have received their reward in full. When you pray, go into your room, close the door and pray to your Father, who is unseen. Then your Father, who sees what is done in secret, will reward you. And when you pray, do not keep on babbling like pagans, for they think they will be heard because of their many words. Do not be like them, for your Father knows what you need before you ask him (Mt 6:5–8).

The Jews were by nature a religious people, who lived in and around the worship of their God. From an early age they were all familiar with the concept and practice of prayer. Every day in the temple, prayers were offered, and as with most religions the leaders were regarded as the main proponents of prayer. The fact that Jesus was a man of prayer was not in itself a surprising thing. Most rabbis with a school of disciples had their own principles and formulas for prayer.

A read through the Gospels shows the primacy of

prayer in Jesus' life. He prayed when he was baptised by John in the River Jordan. He was at prayer on the Mount of Transfiguration. So intense was his prayer in the Garden of Gethsemane that he sweat drops of blood. Quite often, he got up early in the morning before daybreak to spend time with God. All these incidents, however, still don't mark Jesus' prayer life as much different from his peers. What *does* separate him from everyone else was the *way* in which he prayed. Prayer to Jesus was founded in relationship. There was a sense of deep intimacy that permeated his prayer and prayer life. He frequently contrasted the loud self-aggrandising prayers of the Pharisees, who loved to be heard and seen, with the tender honesty and brokenness of those who seemed to be unlikely candidates for heartfelt prayer, such as the tax collector who came to the temple pounding his chest.

Having walked with Jesus, the disciples must have recognised a correlation between his times of prayer and the great displays of wisdom and power that ensued. They came to Jesus after a time and asked him to teach them to pray. As Jews, they must have had a familiarity with prayer, but there was something about Jesus' prayer life they desired. He prefaced his answer with a challenge to humility and honesty. He urged them not to pray to be noticed or to think that God is impressed with great but empty words. 'This is how you should pray: "Our Father . . ."' (Mt 6:9ff). What we have come to call the Lord's Prayer is not really his prayer or particularly a form to pray, but more a starting point to build a relationship with God. When Jesus prayed, he prayed without rules and regulations and prayed simply as a worshipful Son to a loving Father. He emphasised that prayer is not some cosmic manipulation to get one's way, but challenged his followers to yearn for the manifestation of God's kingdom in their midst. He also told a couple of stories to emphasise God's willingness to meet needs. (Surely if your sleepy, grumpy neighbour will get up in the middle of the night because of your persistence, your loving heavenly Father will respond to your needs as you bring them to him?)

On another occasion, Jesus told the story of a widow seeking justice for a good cause and being unable to find it because of the corruptness of the judge. It was not uncommon for judges to receive bribes, and it was rare for a widow to have to present her own case in court. But Jesus told that the woman won her case because of her persistence. The judge was afraid that she would never give him rest. Again, Jesus was reminding his followers that even in tough times, if we keep pressing we will triumph in the end because we serve a loving heavenly Father and can therefore come to him confidently.

Jesus also used prayer to demonstrate his concern for others, not simply in his healing ministry and prayer for the sick, but also for his friends. 'Simon, Simon, Satan has asked to sift you as wheat. But I have prayed for you, Simon, that your faith may not fail' (Lk 22:31–32).

Jesus' prayer life was the product of a love for God and a desire to do his will. Had it not been for the times of prayer, Jesus would never have been able to hear so clearly the voice of the Father and do his works on the earth.

12

Kingdoms in Conflict

We built this city on rock and roll (Starship).

Two cities have been formed by two loves: the earthly by the love of self, even to the contempt of God; the heavenly by the love of God, even to the contempt of self. The former, in a word, glories in itself, the latter in the Lord. The one lifts up its head in its own glory; the other says to its God, 'Thou art my glory and the lifter up of mine head.' In the one, the princes and the nations it subdues are ruled by the love of ruling; in the other, the princes and subjects serve one another in love, the latter obeying, while the former take thought for all. The one delights in its own strength, represented in the persons of its rulers; the other says to its God, 'I love Thee O Lord my strength' (Ron Boehme).[16]

Why did it seem that Jesus' ministry, if truly he was the Messiah, was not totally and immediately successful? It would appear that even some of his closest friends and family struggled to reconcile his apparent failure to bring about the kingdom. It was commonly accepted and expected among the Jews that the Messiah would come and overthrow the oppressors. Struggling under Roman subjugation, the Jew longed for the Messiah to come in keeping with Daniel's prophecies that he would come in might and power to establish his kingdom. Because of his constant antagonism towards the varying sects of religious leaders there was a growing movement against him. Even those who despised each other and were divided on various theological postures, started to come together to seek to put an end to this uncultured upstart from Galilee. His healing ministry was continually undermined. When the common people, in astonishment at the healing of a demon-possessed man who was both dumb and blind, asked the question, 'Could this be the Son of David?' (or in other words the Messiah), the Pharisees attributed his power to the devil.

In Matthew 13, there seems to be somewhat of a turning point in Jesus' ministry, especially in the area of teaching. Perhaps in response to the refusal of many to acknowledge the validity of his person and the rejection, especially among the religious leadership, of his ministry, Jesus began to draw more direct parallels between the seeming insignificance of his ministry and the kingdom he proclaimed, and the actual insignificance of the existing religious institutions in the light of his coming. Although a line had been drawn between him and the religious leaders, he was still a man of the people and the crowds still flocked to meet him. To a crowd that Matthew records as so immense that Jesus was driven from the lakeside and had to take a boat in order to teach, Jesus began to outline some of the reasons why his ministry was not perhaps as immediately successful as expected. He told them the Parable of the Sower and the seed.

A farmer went out to sow his seed. As he was scattering the seed, some fell along the path, and the birds came and ate it up. Some fell on rocky places, where it did not have much soil. It sprang up quickly, because the soil was shallow. But when the sun came up, the plants were scorched, and they withered because they had no root. Other seed fell among thorns, which grew up and choked the plants. Still other seed fell on good soil, where it produced a crop—a hundred, sixty or thirty times what was sown. He who has ears, let him hear (Mt 13:3–9).

To an agricultural society, his story would have been very familiar. The problems of sowing were commonplace, but Jesus used the story to talk about his preaching and the responses to his message. He used the story to explain the apparent ineffectiveness of his kingdom. The sower going out and throwing his precious seed into the fields was at once weak and unimpressive as the seed is insignificant and vulnerable, but on the other hand this was the beginning of a great and significant harvest. Jesus likened his ministry to such a sowing: apparently ineffective and certainly vulnerable to rejection, yet still the seed of the great and mighty kingdom of God. Jesus' seed was his word. He didn't depend on a mighty army or political or economic power to bring about his kingdom, but simply on telling people about the kingdom and inviting them to join in. Of course, he displayed moments of great power, healings and the feeding of thousands miraculously, but those were not the seeds of the kingdom, merely the life of the kingdom at work in the world. Jesus came as Messiah, not to conquer by force or to display other worldly power, but to conquer and establish his kingdom by love. As the seed brought the harvest, so Jesus' words would produce the life of the kingdom.

He talked about the hazards of sowing in this manner; that while all of the seed was good, where it landed and how it was received played a significant role. This made sense to the listeners, who were used to planting crops. Seed that was wasted, seed that fell into bad soil, seed that was choked out by weeds—this was the vulnerability involved in order to reap a harvest. Jesus explained the seeming ineffectiveness of his ministry, not to make excuses, but rather to challenge the listeners as to the kind of 'soil' they might be. It was an invitation to see the kingdom in Jesus, and also an exhortation to consider where they might fit into the picture.

> The disciples came to him and asked, 'Why do you speak to the people in parables?'
> He replied, 'The knowledge of the secrets of the kingdom of heaven has been given to you, but not to them. Whoever has will be given more, and he will have an abundance. Whoever does not have, even what he has will be taken from him' (Mt 13:10–12).

Jesus was ready and willing to open up the heart of the kingdom to those who were seriously seeking truth. But where there was no real vision or confidence in his message and ministry, his illustrations would serve as a repellant. Those who were indifferent would turn away because they would not understand the heart of his message. One had to dig and also to be looking for truth in order to hear in the words of Jesus the voice of eternity. Jesus pinpointed the heart of the problem: callousness. The people had closed their ears and hearts to the truth of the kingdom.

He perhaps best encapsulated the kingdom with his parable about the mustard seed:

The kingdom of heaven is like a mustard seed, which a man took and planted in his field. Though it is the smallest of all your seeds, yet when it grows, it is the largest of the garden plants and becomes a tree, so that the birds of the air come and perch in its branches (Mt 13:31–32).

'Like a mustard seed' was a proverbial way of referring to something really small. Yet from this tiny seed, an amazing plant would grow up to six feet in one season, and be sturdy enough for the birds to rest in. Many expected the kingdom to be all powerful, but Jesus likened it to this tiny seed with amazing growth potential. It was a challenging picture to see in the man from Galilee the seed of a kingdom so powerful and all-embracing that it would touch the very ends of the world.

It was a disappointment to those who awaited the kingdom and looked for might, power and great influence in the world, but those who stayed close to the prophets could see in these fragile, vulnerable beginnings the marks of greatness. Jesus proclaimed a kingdom founded by love, built on tears, forged with humility and led by servanthood. 'For my eyes have seen your salvation, which you have prepared in the sight of all people, a light for revelation to the Gentiles and for glory to your people Israel' (Lk 2:30–32).

Jesus told his disciples that they were blessed at what they were witnessing, for many prophets and righteous men had longed to see what they saw. Isaiah, whom Jesus quoted among these parables, prophesied perhaps more closely than any other of the Old Testament prophets the nature of the Messiah. Hundreds of years before the birth of

Jesus, he had brought forth the visions of the suffering Servant King who would rule, not with force but with justice; who would come as an innocent lamb and die a silent violent death on behalf of all mankind. There was such majesty in his visions, such a closeness, such a capturing of the very essence of Jesus' person and ministry, and yet it was a dream and vision that he never saw realised in his lifetime. And now, the very Messiah dwelling among his people was invisible to eyes blinded by religion and tradition.

13

The Call of the Master

'Cause in this life we make our choices, serve ourselves, or walk in the footsteps of love (Mike Stand, *Footsteps of Love*).[17]

One doesn't discover new lands without consenting to lose sight of the shore for a very long time (André Gide).

As Jesus was walking beside the Sea of Galilee, he saw two brothers, Simon called Peter and his brother Andrew. They were casting a net into the lake, for they were fishermen. 'Come, follow me,' Jesus said, 'and I will make you fishers of men.' At once they left their nets and followed him (Mt 4:18–20).

Jesus went up into the hills and called to him those he wanted, and they came to him (Mk 3:13).

By the middle of the eighteenth century, much of the fire of the Reformation had long been quenched. As mentioned at the beginning of this book, in Great Britain and the rest of Europe Christianity lay like a superficial glaze over the nations. Very few inroads had been made with regard to taking the gospel to other nations of the earth. The missionaries who survived the nightmare journeys to foreign fields were usually met by hostile peoples or diseases which their bodies were not equipped to fight. It seemed that the gospel was being swallowed up and overtaken in the new Age of Reason. But something then happened, and in less than a century there was an explosion of Christian work and mission across the face of the globe. How did it happen? Something occurred in the hearts of men. They caught again the vision of eternity and the voice of God found in the pages of Scripture, and the church was once more drawn into the eternal purposes of God. Men of social standing and public notoriety, as well as common men, suddenly appeared on the front pages of society, proclaiming with passion and fire the gospel of Jesus. Why? For the same reason that Peter and his brother left their nets; left everything. It was that voice. The voice that calls men to follow him. That voice uprooted their lives and for ever changed their perspective. They were never to be the same again.

Even when times became tough for the disciples and things didn't seem to be working out the way they had imagined, and even the crowds that had followed Jesus so faithfully were thinning out, Peter summed up the sentiment of the disciples. They may have been bewildered by many of the things that Jesus spoke about, but one thing they knew for sure was that Jesus had the words of eternal life and there was nowhere else to go. The amazing thing is that when Jesus calls, he lays out no plan. 'Follow me' were the words he used to call his disciples. Nothing else. There was no future laid out before them. No promised salary, no health plan. Just those words. Those words sum up the cost of the call to follow Jesus in a world that plans and has agendas.

Jesus invites us to follow him on the journey into the riches of the kingdom. They left everything. 'All', the Bible says—all that was familiar, the security of their fishing, the riches of the tax collecting business, homes and family. They set out on an uncharted journey that held no visible security for any of them. They attached all their hopes and dreams for life on Jesus and set out to walk the dusty roads of Galilee with the Master. 'For the sake of the call . . .' sings one contemporary Christian artist, and that was the essence of the disciples' choice. They gave up everything upon hearing those words. It wasn't a neat theological assessment or decision. It was a choice to make themselves one with Jesus; to discover their own identities as they discovered his.

> As they were walking along the road, a man said to him, 'I will follow you wherever you go.'
>
> Jesus replied, 'Foxes have holes and birds of the air have nests, but the Son of Man has no place to lay his head.'
>
> He said to another man, 'Follow me.'
>
> But the man replied, 'Lord, first let me go and bury my father.'
>
> Jesus said to him, 'Let the dead bury their own dead, but you go and proclaim the kingdom of God.'
>
> Still another said, 'I will follow you, Lord; but first let me go back and say good-bye to my family.'
>
> Jesus replied, 'No-one who puts his hand to the plough and looks back is fit for service in the kingdom of God' (Lk 9:57–62).

This teaching is found in a very important chapter about the nature of Jesus' kingdom. This situation occurred as Jesus was walking along the road with his disciples. He alone understood the times; that the time was approaching for him to be taken up to heaven. But for him it would not be the chariot of fire that collected the prophet Elijah, whom Jesus had recently talked to on a mountainside (Lk 9:30). For Jesus, being taken up to heaven meant the horror of the cross. However, Jesus had set out for Jerusalem in a determined manner, even though the journey announced the beginning of the end.

As they were walking, a man approached Jesus and declared his desire to follow him. 'I will follow you wherever you go,' he said. He had not been called or recruited, but he wanted to join in. Perhaps he had been drawn by the force of mission, or had been enthralled by the miracle ministry of Jesus. We don't know the reason, but Jesus' response was quick and hard: 'Foxes have holes and birds of the air have nests, but the Son of Man has no place to lay his head.' The man wanted to join, but he had no understanding of what it really meant to follow Jesus. He had no comprehension that to follow the man from Galilee meant Gethsemane and Golgotha. The Jews of Jesus' day were awaiting their Messiah, but the idea of following a rejected, suffering Messiah would have been an incredible shock. Jesus' reply was not a harsh rejection, but a harsh reality, and he was saying in essence that whatever your motive, consider the fact that the man you desire to follow will be despised and rejected of men. We are not told the outcome of the encounter. There is no answer from the man who volunteered. We don't know if on the basis of new information he was still as eager to join the company or whether he dropped back to the side of the road and allowed Jesus and his entourage to travel on without him. This incident is a reminder to any who would volunteer to follow Jesus without serious assessment of the cost of such a decision and what it really means to follow a suffering, rejected Master.

The next man introduced into the scenario was not a volunteer but a recruit. Jesus extended to this man the same words that he extended to the men who now walked with him along the road: 'Follow me.' This man wanted to follow Jesus, but he made a request. He wanted to go and bury his father first. Without an understanding of Jewish culture, one could read Jesus' response and consider it quite heartless: 'Let the dead bury their own dead, but you go and proclaim the kingdom of God.' The nature of the man's request does not necessarily mean that his father was literally dead, but in their culture it was regarded as a son's duty to serve and help his parents until they died. He was faced with the choice of fulfilling the expectations of his cultural community life or answering the call.

There was always a sense of urgency that permeated the life and ministry of Jesus. Not a desperate rash hurriedness that painted a picture of a man driven by circumstances and hurriedly trying to achieve his goals, but an urgency of a man on a divine mission who understood the frailty of time and the need for men to respond now. The recruit asked, 'Do you expect me to violate my traditional responsibilities?' Jesus' response exclaimed 'Yes!' It was a call to proclaim the kingdom; an invitation extended to be part of the advancing of God's purposes as a present reality. Jesus said the spiritually dead could take care of the cultural and traditional responsibilities, but as for you—and there was emphasis on the 'you'—go and proclaim the arrival of the kingdom. Again we are not told of the response. Often with the teachings and parables of

Jesus the open-ended manner in which they leave the reader hanging is done purposely. This, I believe, is in order to challenge the reader to ask himself the same questions.

One more man entered the picture—another volunteer. He made the same determined offer to follow Jesus, and although he had a small precondition, it seemed insignificant and a legitimate request. He simply wanted to go and say good-bye to his family. After all, it was unlikely that he knew Jesus and his company were going to be passing by, and simply to disappear down the road with Jesus could have had terrible effects on his family, who would have had no idea of his whereabouts. There was also historic precedence for the request. After all, even Elisha had asked for time to say farewell to his family before he joined Elijah, and it was granted to him. However, once again it was more than a simple good-bye; it reads more literally 'to take leave of'. In Jesus' time, the person leaving was supposed to request permission from those who were staying. The man was saying that he desired to follow Jesus and wanted to go and get permission first—a questionable approach indeed. The likelihood of finding a favourable response to such a request was dim to say the least. Jesus' answer was once again short and to the point: 'No-one who puts his hand to the plough and looks back is. fit for service in the kingdom of God.'

The ploughs common to that time were very light and had to be kept upright with just the right amount of pressure in order to regulate the depth of the furrow. The ploughman steered the plough with one hand and the oxen with the other. It was important that he kept his eyes between the oxen in order to keep the furrow straight. He also had to look out for rocks which could damage the blade should he not be aware of their location. If a ploughman was distracted, he could break the plough and ruin the field. It was also common for a ploughman to work in a team, so if he did a bad job it wasn't simply his own work he was destroying but the livelihood of others as well. The ploughman worked over ploughing already done and often before work yet to be done. In using this analogy, Jesus was saying that whoever wished to follow him had to be resolved and to break every link with the past and commit his life to the coming kingdom of God. The person caught between the tension of conflicting loyalties; who was constantly distracted by what once was, was useless to the kingdom. Divided loyalty would not only be unproductive but ultimately destructive to both him and other labourers.

The call of God challenges us to cut off our past life. It may not be that, as with Simon or Matthew, we must leave our occupation, but at the very least the call will challenge our perspective and priorities in life.

> Elisha then left his oxen and ran after Elijah. 'Let me kiss my father and mother good-bye,' he said, 'and then I will come with you.'
>
> 'Go back,' Elijah replied. 'What have I done to you?'
>
> So Elisha left him and went back. He took his yoke of oxen and slaughtered them. He burned the ploughing equipment to cook the meat and gave it to the people, and they ate. Then he set out to follow Elijah and became his attendant (1 Kings 19:20–21).

The call of God uproots, overthrows and challenges all that is familiar. Elisha left the plough, Abraham left the city, Peter left his nets and Matthew his money. There has been a definite lack in much of the Christian church in the latter half of this century, in its proclamation of the call. Many invite people to follow Jesus without challenging them to the changes that being a follower necessitates. In many instances Jesus has been portrayed as a really nice person whom one can simply tack on to the end of one's life. But to follow him demands change. Abraham left the city to look for another one, whose builder and maker was God. The call upon his life demanded movement in directions that he had never considered before. He left the security of all that was familiar to him in Ur and spent the rest of his life on a journey, while all around him settled into routine. 'Get out!' were the words that uprooted Abraham. The same words challenged the heart of Gladys Aylward who set out to work in China, even after being told by legitimate mission societies that she was not qualified to serve. She could be denied by man, but she could not deny the call of Jesus upon her life.

'Follow me' are simple words, but words that demand obedience; words that require movement and words that also bring change, along with great adventure: 'Foxes have holes . . . but the Son of Man has nowhere to lay his head.'

In the story of the three men, Jesus said first that the Son of Man was not the victorious, triumphant figure one would expect—he walked the path of sorrows. Are we willing to walk that way with him? Secondly, loyalty to Jesus and his kingdom is far more important than the demands of the norms in society, and, more than that, the demands of our culture are not acceptable excuses for failure in discipleship. And thirdly, there can be no distractions. The call takes precedence. Why so difficult? It would seem that things could be much smoother without so many taxing obligations, but it is important to understand the nature of the relationship between Master and disciple. Kenneth Bailey puts it this way:

> A part of the tension of the dialogue is the underlying assumption of the necessarily close relationship between a disciple and his teacher. In the Middle East such a relationship has always been deep and binding. The Talmud states that 'A father and his son or a master and his disciple . . are regarded as one individual' (B. T. Erubin 73a, Sonc., 510). Becoming the student/disciple of a sage is not a simple matter of 'signing up for a course' for the purpose of acquiring information. Rather it is the cementing of a lifelong relationship to a person. With this as an understood starting point Jesus is here demanding that his authority (the demands of the kingdom) take precedence over all other relationships (Kenneth E. Bailey).[18]

In this age in which we pride ourselves on the information available to us about any and all subjects, the call of Jesus stands in opposition. Discipleship is not the accumulation of data and information about Jesus Christ, or even hero worship. It is relationship with him, characterised by obedience. It is not the challenge to know the geographical locations where he walked, but rather following him—putting our feet in his footsteps and walking with him in a broken world.

14

No Sacrifice

For my own part, I have never ceased to rejoice that God has appointed me to such an office. People talk of the sacrifice I have made in spending so much of my life in Africa. Can that be called a sacrifice which is simply paid back as a small part of a great debt owing to our God, which we can never repay? Is that a sacrifice which brings its own blest reward in healthful activity, the consciousness of doing good, peace of mind, and a bright hope of a glorious destiny hereafter? Away with the word in such a view, and with such a thought! It is emphatically no sacrifice. Say rather it is a privilege. Anxiety, sickness, suffering, or danger, now and then, with a foregoing of the common conveniences and charities of this life, may make us pause, and cause the spirit to waver, and the soul to sink; but let this only be for a moment. All these are nothing when compared with the glory which shall hereafter be revealed in and for us. I never made a sacrifice (David Livingstone).[19]

The privilege to serve Jesus is always higher than the price (Joy Dawson).[20]

Life begins at the cross. It's not easy to take but it's the price you pay. Life begins at the cross no other way (Ric Alba, 'Life Begins at the Cross').[21]

As we've seen, it was the call to follow Jesus that changed the lives of his disciples. That call was not without cost. The kingdom was serious business with Jesus. He was not out to entertain or to tickle the ears of those who gathered to hear him. His words cut to the core of a society set apart by God with incredible promise and destiny. He aggressively confronted the self-serving religious leaders of his day and frequently challenged those who came to him seeking validation for their works. Jesus portrayed the following of God's commands as more than shallow ritual or routine, and he placed great price on the cost of walking with him into the life of the kingdom. He often presented choices in life—simply one thing or the other. In many ways his teaching was a repetition of a thread woven throughout the Old Testament, that life basically condensed down to two choices: life or death. Both Moses and Joshua laid before the children of Israel those same choices. Perhaps it is most succinctly summed up by the prophet Jeremiah: 'This is what the Lord says: See, I am setting before you the way of life and the way of death' (Jer 21:8).

Jesus presented the kingdom in much the same way. Many of his parables highlighted the choices: the two roads, good and bad fruit, and many other examples. In Matthew 7:13 Jesus had this to say about the kingdom: 'Enter through the narrow gate. For wide is the gate and broad is the road that leads to destruction, and many enter through it. But small is the gate and narrow the road that leads to life, and only a few find it.'

Although the roads in Jesus' time were nothing compared with our roads today, there were nevertheless a significant number of wide thoroughfares which were the arteries between the main population centres. These were well travelled and well defined. There were also innumerable lesser roads and paths that criss-crossed the land. And there were major gates that provided entrance into and protection for the major cities. Jesus used these two sets of opposites to paint the picture of the cost of entering into the kingdom. The road into the kingdom is less travelled and implies loneliness and vulnerability. Also, it is portrayed by Jesus as difficult. In opposition is the well-travelled road that most people choose. On that road you will find many more travelling companions, and the journey will, at least in the beginning, be much more enjoyable. But Jesus also alluded to the fact that both roads have different destinations. The wide road leads to destruction and sadly many journey that way, ignorant of the desperate path they are travelling. In contrast, those willing to pay the price and journey on the narrow road find life in the end.

This and many other parables painted the picture of the cost of the kingdom. The price is different for every individual. For the rich young ruler in Matthew 13, his challenge was not simply to do just one more thing to find life. He had to weigh up all of his life and learn that it wasn't mere regard for law God was looking for, but complete whole-hearted commitment to the cause of God. Jesus challenged him to sell all his goods, then give the money to the poor and follow Jesus. This was a high price for a wealthy man to pay, but again, there could be no distractions. The kingdom is not a game—it is serious business—and Jesus had no time for those who came to him looking for approval. One of the most harrowing symbols of the cost of discipleship is the cross. On many occasions Jesus mentioned the cross as the price of following him.

That analogy must have struck fear into the hearts of many people. Living under Roman occupation, the cross as a means of torturous death was a familiar sight to them, and yet Jesus chose this as the cost of following him. As Dietrich Bonhoeffer said so well, 'When Christ calls a man, he bids him come and die.'[22]

In Luke 14, Jesus pronounced one of his great crowd-thinning statements: 'If anyone comes to me and does not hate his father and mother, his wife and children, his brothers and sisters—yes, even his own life—he cannot be my disciple. And anyone who does not carry his cross and follow me cannot be my disciple' (vv 26–27). Jesus was not stating that the mark of Christian discipleship is hatred of those who are nearest and dearest, for that would have been a violation of the heart of the law that demanded honour to parents and care for family. It was rather a challenge to priority, because at times those closest can be the greatest hindrance to following Jesus. Even personal goals, dreams and desires can cloud the issues. Jesus was not so much interested in the street-level popularity that he was gaining, but rather in portraying the importance of the kingdom and the high priority that it must have in the human heart.

In an age of immediacy such as ours, where we microwave everything and impatiently wait for the two-minute bell, Jesus challenges even our presentation of the gospel. In a society that looks for immediate results and success, Jesus challenges us all to weigh the implications of following him in the kingdom. He continued in Luke 14:28–35:

> Suppose one of you wants to build a tower. Will he not first sit down and estimate the cost to see if he has

enough money to complete it? For if he lays the
foundation and is not able to finish it, everyone who
sees it will ridicule him, saying, 'This fellow began to
build and was not able to finish.'

Or suppose a king is about to go to war against
another king. Will he not first sit down and consider
whether he is able with ten thousand men to oppose the
one coming against him with twenty thousand? If he is
not able, he will send a delegation while the other is still
a long way off and will ask for terms of peace. In the
same way, any of you who does not give up everything
he has cannot be my disciple.

Salt is good, but if it loses its saltiness, how can it be
made salty again? It is fit neither for the soil nor for the
manure heap; it is thrown out.

He who has ears to hear, let him hear.

Here Jesus talks about weighing up the cost. It
requires meditation and consideration, and he
likens the decision to a builder and a king, both of
whom face serious situations. First, Jesus likens the
decision to the task of a builder, who must consider
whether or not he has the resources to finish the
building, because the builder who fails to calculate
the cost in advance and goes broke halfway through
appears foolish. But the more serious situation is the
one of the king facing war. It is vital that he
considers the cost of battle. If it is clear that he
cannot win, it is imperative that he make peace with
his enemies quickly in order to avoid total devas-
tation. Jesus speaks of the need to weigh up the cost
of the undertaking. And what is that cost for anyone
who chooses to respond to the call? Jesus said that it
is many things: taking up a cross, hating your own
life, considering the price. Ultimately, it is the fact
that priority in life must be given to kingdom issues

and activity. In no way can following Jesus be a part-time activity; it requires and calls for total commitment. Not just to the kingdom, but to the King himself.

At times the teachings of Jesus seem to be opposite to many of the claims of the church. We have condensed the Sermon on the Mount to a series of 'be happy' attitudes, which seem lightweight and trite, especially since one of the supposed happy attitudes is mourning! We have proclaimed Christ as Saviour and reiterated over and over the need to be 'born again'. While I fully believe in the need for and the claims of Scripture regarding new birth, I feel that we must also reconsider that Jesus only once said a man had to be born again, but time and again throughout the pages of the gospel he called men to follow him. I believe that to follow Jesus involves more than simply reciting a prayer and feeling a warm glow. It is ultimately a weighed decision to commit ourselves to living a life given to and shaped by Christ. I sense that much of our understanding and proclamation of the kingdom does little to prepare people for what, at times, can be the harsh realities of kingdom living. 'Foxes have holes and birds have nests . . .' was a statement Jesus made, and it is seldom acknowledged today in the midst of a gospel society that is often affected by the materialistic world in which it finds itself.

There is definitely a sombre thread running through many of Jesus' teachings, and they can at times be traumatising. The idea of traipsing around Galilee sounds like fun provided that there is a warm hotel bed at the end of the day. Having grown up in western society, we have become accustomed to a level of comfort unknown in human history, and that lends all the more weight to the words of Jesus.

However, while Jesus did not minimise the cost of following him, he did not neglect the other side of the story, which is the benefit of following him. In Mark 10, Jesus was approached by a young man who asked an incredibly important question: 'What must I do to inherit eternal life?'

Although his question appears noble, there is also a hint of self-righteousness in the question. Jesus responded by giving him an obvious answer: obedience to the command of God is where eternal life is found. But the young man was not really seeking the answer; he was looking for something more which he could do to impress God. After a discussion about which commands to obey, the young man said that he had kept them all faithfully since he was a boy. Mark then says that Jesus 'looked at him and loved him' and then said, 'One thing you lack. Go, sell everything you have and give to the poor, and you will have treasure in heaven. Then come, follow me.' Jesus proclaimed in essence that to follow him is to obey all the commands of the law. The young man was not prepared to pay this price because it required total renunciation of all his ways and the loss of his substantial income. And with sadness, he departed.

Jesus turned to his disciples and made a statement about how difficult it is for rich people to enter the kingdom. In fact, he said that it is easier for a camel to go through the eye of a needle. Needless to say, the disciples were concerned and began to wonder who, if anyone, could find salvation. Jesus comforted them with the promise of God's power to do the impossible, and then Peter spoke up to remind

Jesus that though they were perhaps not wealthy, they had paid the price, considered the cost of following him. Jesus replied with words of great promise:

> I tell you the truth . . . no-one who has left home or brothers or sisters or mother or father or children or fields for me and the gospel will fail to receive a hundred times as much in this present age (homes, brothers, sisters, mothers, children and fields—and with them, persecutions) and in the age to come, eternal life (Mk 10:29–30).

Jesus proclaimed that the kingdom was one of great cost, but also filled with great joy. He said that it was impossible to give more to God than God would give to you. Perhaps two of the most insightful parables into this area are found in the thirteenth chapter of Matthew. As we have said, although discipleship is costly, the rewards are incalculable and the joy unspeakable.

> The kingdom of heaven is like treasure hidden in a field. When a man found it, he hid it again, and then in his joy went and sold all he had and bought that field.
> Again, the kingdom of heaven is like a merchant looking for fine pearls. When he found one of great value, he went away and sold everything he had and bought it (Mt 13:44–46).

As mentioned earlier, it was common in times when there were no safety deposit boxes or vaults, for people to hide their valuables in the ground. In contrast to the cost, Jesus paints the reward and joy of the kingdom as similar to coming across unexpected treasure or discovering a pearl so beautiful that it makes all others seem pale and worthless in comparison. Discipleship *is* costly, but it brings rewards that nothing else can, and a joy that is utterly 'other worldly'. To commit your life to the kingdom is to be taken out of your own little puddle and dropped into the immense ocean of God's kingdom.

Jesus called twelve men whose world up until that time consisted of a few square miles of middle-eastern desert, and he commissioned them to encompass the whole world in the service of his kingdom. To respond to the call is to find shape and meaning to life that is impossible to find outside commitment to the kingdom. To hold on to anything in preference to the kingdom is to prefer a fake pearl to a real one. Jim Elliot, a great missionary pioneer and fiery disciple of Jesus, who met his death at the hands of the very Indians to whom he had gone to proclaim the treasure, said it best: 'He is no fool who gives up what he cannot keep to gain what he cannot lose.'[23] There is no greater reward in this life than to live and labour for things beyond yourself, things eternal, things of the kingdom.

15

How the Kingdom Works

Welcome to the MS-DOS operating system, version 4.0. If you are new at working with operating systems for personal computers, you will want to learn a few basics before you go on to learn about the advanced features of MS-DOS. This MS-DOS User's Guide was written to help you understand the fundamentals of using MS-DOS with your personal computer.[24]

When the disciples James and John saw this, they asked, 'Lord, do you want us to call fire down from heaven to destroy them?' But Jesus turned and rebuked them. And he said, 'You do not know what kind of spirit you are of, for the Son of Man did not come to destroy men's lives, but to save them' (Lk 9:54–55).

The Apostle Paul thought he had it right, but in fact he had it all wrong. As a Jew, he had spent his life trying to prove himself righteous before God. He made bold claims about his ability to live up to the demands of the law. He himself said that with respect to legalistic righteousness, he was faultless. But everything changed when he met Christ and he spent the rest of his days not attempting perfectionism or self-righteous religion, but living out the call of Christ. Perhaps more than any other New

101

Testament writer, he had a grasp of the work of grace upon him, and he continually challenged the church to remain close to its founder and head. In Philippians, he laid out a challenge to those new converts *and* to us, in order that we might let people know what God is really like. God provided himself with no avenue other than the church by which to communicate himself to mankind.

> Your attitude should be the same as that of Christ Jesus: Who, being in very nature God, did not consider equality with God something to be grasped, but made himself nothing, taking the very nature of a servant, being made in human likeness. And being found in appearance as a man, he humbled himself and became obedient to death—even death on a cross! Therefore God exalted him to the highest place (Phil 2:5–8).

These words not only present the lordship of Jesus, which was attained through the cross, but also demonstrate the fruit of his willingness to become as a man, humbling himself and dying the death of the cross. Paul's words declare that in all of the universe, there is no person of higher authority, and he arrived at that place by taking the path of servanthood. This was written to a church established in a Roman colony, aware of the might and power by which Rome exercised authority. In many ways it was a world much like ours, where dominance is the means by which men rule. To understand how the kingdom of heaven works, we must first at least attempt to grasp the fact that the Son of God came into our midst as a man and didn't see the glory of his majesty as something to be held onto. He made himself nothing, Paul says. He emptied himself of all his rights and came to wash the feet of a dirty world. The enormity of that is almost incomprehensible.

There is a famous fresco in Italy that portrays the hand of man reaching out to the finger of God. In the artwork, the distance between the two seems very small, but in reality it was vast and impossible to cross for man. Into that chasm stepped Jesus, bridging the gap between the Creator and his beloved creation and he achieved it by servanthood. Everything about Jesus' life demonstrated and manifested the 'emptying' that Paul spoke of. To step from the throne of heaven to be born a baby in a barn, in an anonymous city; to have a common name and be raised in an area of Israel not renowned for producing anything good; to own nothing more than the clothes he wore on his back; to be surrounded by suspect people; and in the end, to journey alone to a cross deserted by all—these are the cornerstones of the kingdom.

The disciples continually struggled to grasp the things that Jesus spoke to them concerning the kingdom. They jockeyed for position, manoeuvred for power and favour and even argued among themselves as to which of them was the 'greatest'. On one occasion, two of the disciples brought their mothers along with them to talk to Jesus about potential promotion. They probably figured that a mother's request would touch Jesus' heart, but Jesus told them that they did not know what they were asking for. When the other ten disciples got wind of what had occurred, they were upset—probably because they didn't ask *their* mothers to help. Once again, Jesus had to remind them of the nature of his upside-down kingdom:

You know that the rulers of the Gentiles lord it over them, and their high officials exercise authority over them. Not so with you. Instead, whoever wants to become great among you must be your servant, and whoever wants to be first must be your slave—just as the Son of Man did not come to be served, but to serve, and to give his life as a ransom for many (Mt 20:25–28).

'Not so among you' were Jesus' watchwords to his followers. He called them not to be like the religious leaders, who were noted for their hypocrisy—who, while claiming to serve God, were simply serving themselves, and in every aspect of their lives portrayed the opposite spirit to the kingdom which they proclaimed. He also challenged them not to be like the Gentile rulers, who loved to exercise power and lord it over other people. The kingdoms of the world are characterised by power, isolation and unapproachability, but Jesus' kingdom must be noted for being vulnerable, available and approachable. Jesus could be touched and came to put us in touch with God. He went everywhere reaching out and ministering to people. The world has seen no greater power than that of Jesus, and he calls us to exercise the same power by living out his loving servant lifestyle.

Jesus' ministry style was counter-cultural, trans-cultural and pro-cultural. He introduced images and possibilities not conceived within the culture. His was not a ministry of asceticism. His lifestyle is not about promotion but demotion; it's not about advancing but diminishing. It's about dying to self, that God's life might be ministered to others. While human nature is about reaching to heights, the kingdom of heaven points down. Jesus stepped down from the riches of heaven's throne and wrapped himself in the towel of a servant, laying aside heaven for earth. The Pharisees accused Jesus of many things—drinking and eating too much, associating with the wrong types, saying the wrong things—but they could never accuse him of not loving and serving humanity.

His whole life was directed towards others. He lived with a desire to see men set free from bondage and sin. At the end of his life it seemed that his enemies had won. His closest friends had deserted him, and the cheers of the crowd had become screams of hatred and uncontrolled violence. Nailed to a tree with his life agonisingly draining from him, with soldiers gambling for his clothing and a heartless crowd mocking him, there was nothing left of any outward influence about his life that could in any way grip the hearts of men.

> One of the criminals who hung there hurled insults at him: 'Aren't you the Christ? Save yourself and us!'
> But the other criminal rebuked him. 'Don't you fear God,' he said, 'since you are under the same sentence? We are punished justly, for we are getting what our deeds deserve. But this man has done nothing wrong.'
> Then he said, 'Jesus, remember me when you come into your kingdom.'
> Jesus answered him, 'I tell you the truth, today you will be with me in paradise' (Lk 23:39–43).

If ever Isaiah's words were true that Jesus would have no beauty or majesty to attract us to him and nothing in his appearance that would cause us to desire him, it must have been as he hung on the cross. Rather than the attempts of some Romantic artists to soften the reality, the fact is that crucifixion was a horrible way to die. And, added to that, Jesus had been whipped to the bone, crowned with thorns, beaten about the face and finally hammered onto a tree with heavy Roman nails. And yet at that moment, when the world had done its worst, there was something about the man that caused a dying thief to look into his eyes and honour him as King.

He emptied himself of heaven's glory and walked the earth in service to mankind. The starting point in his kingdom is to understand that he calls us to serve the world with love, and to empty ourselves of any attitude that might hinder us in that mission.

16

In the Name of Love

All you need is love (The Beatles).

Love is a wonderful thing (Michael Bolton).

I've seen love conquer the great divide (U2).

A new commandment I give you: Love one another. As I have loved you, so you must love one another. All men will know that you are my disciples if you love one another (Jn 13:34–35).

If the kingdom is advanced by servanthood, it must be characterised by love. Jesus Christ was love incarnate, love made flesh. He came to show the world the loving heart of the Father God and he expressed love in every conceivable way. His was love without condition, bias or qualification. To a world that sought to limit its obligations, Jesus threw open his arms and embraced all. He came to a people who were challenged with two types of love: the love of God with all of their heart, soul and might; and to the love of neighbour as they loved themselves. To this society Jesus brought a new example of love; a love that went beyond neighbourly love.

At the end of things, as his earthly ministry was

drawing to a close and the plot to kill him had already been initiated, Jesus called together his disciples and shared a final feast with them. 'Having loved his own who were in the world, he now showed them the full extent of his love' (Jn 13:1). That night, as he washed their feet and shared bread with the one who was to betray him with the kiss of a friend, he laid before his closest friends a new command, upon which his kingdom would be hinged and by which his followers would be recognised. This new standard was not simply neighbourly love, but to love as *he* had loved them. Some say that Christian love is more than a feeling—that it is a duty. However, Christ's love was not perfunctory obedience, but the manifestation of God's heart; it was full of emotion and feeling. This love wept, was moved with compassion, mourned over lost friends, and loved deeply even those who rejected him. Christ's love was more than mere words, a pat on the back or empty duty; it was a love that manifested itself in giving itself away.

Jesus calls us all to love as he loved us. It's love with a price, love that sacrifices, but love that ultimately triumphs. It is love that stands in opposition to our world's interpretation of love. This love acknowledges that to love does mean having to say you're sorry. 'You have heard that it was said, "Love your neighbour and hate your enemy." But I tell you, Love your enemies and pray for those who persecute you, that you may be sons of your Father in heaven' (Mt 5:43–45). If we only love those who love us, that does not separate us and make us unique. Jesus calls us to walk in love, even when our enemies seek to triumph over us.

Not only did Jesus establish a new command and

provide a new standard for love relationships, the New Testament writers utilised a little-used Greek word for love: *agape*. Scholars say that the roots of this word are found in the Greek words for victory and conquest. The love that Jesus demonstrated certainly seems to fit those qualifications. In order for victory there must be battle, and by love Jesus waged war against the very powers of hell. In calling us to love one another as he loved us, he challenges us to go to war against the very things that destroy lives and relationships in this world. 'For in Christ Jesus neither circumcision nor uncircumcision has any value. The only thing that counts is faith expressing itself through love' (Gal 5:6).

What does it mean to love? It means different things at different times. In Paul's letter to Philemon he wrote about what this love meant to a slave owner, to a runaway slave and to him personally. Their lives had become intertwined by relationship with Jesus and that bond demanded that they face some very sticky issues. Onesimus, Philemon's slave, had run away, and on his escape had come to Christ, and also been befriended by Paul the apostle. The Roman empire was a society built on and existing by the use of slaves. For a runaway slave the sentence was death, immediate and unavoidable, in order to maintain power over the millions of chained people. This presented quite a predicament for a Christian slave owner and a runaway Christian slave. How could the situation be resolved? Only by love, Paul declares. Love that brings victory.

But it also meant different things to all involved. To Onesimus, the slave, love meant going back and putting right the wrongs. That was an intense demand of love, but if he was to fulfil Jesus' command, he had no choice. For Philemon, the slave owner (pressured to do right by the world's standard, which meant dealing mercilessly with a runaway slave), this love meant yielding to a higher justice and welcoming Onesimus home, not simply as a slave but as a brother in the Lord and relating to him in that light. Ultimately Philemon was challenged to forgive as he had been forgiven. 'I appeal to you on the basis of love' (Philem 9).

In a very difficult situation, Paul challenged all involved with Christ's example of love. He also had to face the ramifications of Christ's command. This runaway slave had found his way not only into the kingdom, but deep into Paul's heart. 'My very heart' is how Paul referred to Onesimus in his letter to Philemon. He could have written to Philemon and railed against slavery, highlighting the insidiousness of owning human beings as you would other goods. But he did not. Instead, he placed Christ's standard of love as the barometer by which to resolve a tense and difficult situation. Paul knew that in sending the slave home, he ran the risk of sending him to his death, but love compelled him and love drew him into the situation. And yet Paul sent him back not simply as a slave, but also as a brother to his former owner. 'By a principle essential to Christianity, a person is eternally differenced from a thing: so that the idea of a human being necessarily excludes the idea of property in that being' (Samuel Taylor Coleridge).[25]

For Paul in this circumstance, love meant getting involved, being willing to stand in the gap and build bridges between broken relationships. Love not only challenged him to stand in the middle, but it cost him something too: 'If he has done you any wrong or owes you anything, charge it to me. . . . I will pay it back' (Philem 18–19). Love meant that Paul became involved, not only in word but with his conscience and his cheque book! Love is always costly. 'For God so loved the world that he gave his one and only Son' (Jn 3:16). God's love for the world conquered death and rose victorious from the grave, but he also paid a terrible price in sacrificing himself for us. To love each other as Christ loved us is not to offer empty Christian platitudes—it involves sacrifice, involvement and cost.

> You have heard that it was said, 'Eye for eye, and tooth for tooth.' But I tell you, Do not resist an evil person. If someone strikes you on the right cheek, turn to him the other also. And if someone wants to sue you and take your tunic, let him have your cloak as well. If someone forces you to go one mile, go with him two miles. Give to the one who asks you, and do not turn away from the one who wants to borrow from you (Mt 5:38–42).

This portion of Scripture is well known and often cited for its incredible insight into the kingdom of God which operates by standards different from the kingdom of men. To turn the other cheek has often been cited as a call to pacifism. In Jesus' time, to be slapped on the cheek was more an insult than a violent crime. The law was given to restrain retaliation, but Jesus in these few examples brings forth the manner in which love responds. To turn the other cheek means to let the insults come and then to respond with grace, not retaliation, because you are a child of heaven.

Also, a Jew's coat was virtually 'holy' to him, and was used in many ways in the culture to conduct business. Men often went to court because someone had not returned their coat. Jesus says in effect, 'Don't make your rights, legal or otherwise, the basis for your relationships with others—let Christ's love be your example.'

The Roman oppressors could force Jewish citizens into service for them and make them walk a certain distance to perform functions. In response to this, Jesus says that when you are compelled to journey a mile, volunteer to go one extra to provide an example of your service to a greater King of a more powerful empire. The role of a servant is to give his life in service to others. Christ's call to love as he loved is a challenge to go beyond the begrudging service of duty into the world of serving with and by love.

17

Incarnational Christianity

I have a dream (Martin Luther King).

I believe in the kingdom come . . . but I still haven't found what I'm looking for (U2).

This is how you should pray: 'Our Father in heaven, hallowed be your name, your kingdom come, your will be done on earth as it is in heaven' (Mt 6:9–10).

In calling his followers to serve the world with love, Jesus was portraying an incarnational faith; a faith with hands and feet. It required a determination to serve in his cause, not merely to hold a belief in his person. His was not to be a religion performed, yet denying the power; it was not to be outwardly holy and yet inwardly corrupt; it was not to say one thing and do another—it was to be characterised by tangible expressions of God's love and mercy. His kingdom followers were to be like their Master, wrapped in a towel washing the dirty feet of the world, giving water to the thirsty, food to the hungry and clothing to the naked. In contrast to the religion of the Pharisees, whose doctrine prevented them from care and drained all compassion from their lives, Jesus called his church to live with kingdom eyes. As the Pharisees concerned themselves with their own agendas, Jesus called his followers to put the concerns of God first.

> 'What do you think? There was a man who had two sons. He went to the first and said, "Son, go and work today in the vineyard."
>
> '"I will not," he answered, but later he changed his mind and went.
>
> 'Then the father went to the other son and said the same thing. He answered, "I will, sir," but he did not go.
>
> 'Which of the two did what his father wanted?'
>
> 'The first,' they answered.
>
> Jesus said to them, 'I tell you the truth, the tax collectors and the prostitutes are entering the kingdom of God ahead of you' (Mt 21:28–31).

In this little story, Jesus highlighted that which God prizes: the obedience of those who fulfil his concern. This story was given in response to the challenge of his authority by the chief priest and elders of Israel. Jesus portrayed them as the one who said he would obey and do the bidding of his father and yet did not. In contrast were the broken sinners, likened to the son who at first rejected the father's request, but then relented and did the work to be done in the father's vineyard. Here Jesus was spotlighting the priority of the kingdom, which is to put the concerns of God first. The Pharisees and other religious leaders had done a good job in stifling the plans and purposes of God by placing their own agendas before his. The world needs a new breed of people—those not armed with their own agendas and theological books tucked under their arms, but men with new hearts that burn for the purposes of God.

Jesus laid out his manifesto, this new order of men, in what is regarded as his greatest dissertation:

the Sermon on the Mount. In this teaching, Jesus contrasts the world's order and agenda with God's. In many ways it stands as an indictment to the religious order of his day, who in their resistance to enter into the fullness of God's kingdom—also by their religion—prevented others from entering. These are the people he described in Matthew 23 as swallowing camels and straining at gnats; the absurdity of those who choose religion over relationship. He lays forth to the assembled people his vision of the world as God intended, filled with people who, in contrast to the self-righteous spirit of man apart from God, are aware of the poverty of their lives without him. These are the ones who can see a completely different kingdom and a different set of rules by which to operate.

Salt and light were two of Jesus' main descriptions of his followers. In a world fast decaying, they were to provide preservation, stopping the decay by the introduction of the kingdom into men's lives. And by reflecting his love in a dark world they were to dispel the works of darkness. A faith of doing as well as being.

Almost half a century ago, an insignificant Albanian nun moved to India and took up residence in an abandoned Hindu temple in Calcutta. She changed the name of the temple to The House of Charity and above the door hung a sign which now hangs over the entrance to the many houses of charity scattered around the globe wherever poverty and disease run rampant. The sign carries two simple words: 'I thirst.' Those two words uttered by Jesus from the cross are the motivating force in Mother Teresa's life and ministry. She understands that to be salt and light involves putting hands and feet to your faith and confronting the reality of hell wherever it is found.

John Wesley said: 'You will preach, bury, you will marry and baptise but you will be imminent failures if you merely perform your role. Your life must encompass true mission.'[26] He understood that the Christian life involved much more than the perfunctory observance of religious ritual, and demanded the upheaval and uprooting of all that was wrong in a society, to the glory of God. We live in a world that has lost its way; that has no sense of the true value of life, and struggles to find shape and meaning for its existence. We must be responsive and sensitive to our generation if we are truly to touch it.

> When I heard this, I tore my tunic and cloak, pulled hair from my head and beard and sat down appalled. Then everyone who trembled at the words of the God of Israel gathered around me because of this unfaithfulness of the exiles. And I sat there appalled until the evening sacrifice (Ez 9:3–4).

I don't know how it happened, but somewhere along the line in the journey of the church, reservation and removal seemed to have become the order of the day, and the church has tended to appear cold and clinical in its emotions. This is a far cry from the prophets, who were broken by the message which they had to carry to a people who had lost their way. But a Christianity, cold and uninspiring, will do little to affect the world which is already characterised by deadness. The Apostle Paul said in the book of Ephesians that we who are Christians have been made alive from the deadness of our lives of sin. What does it mean to be alive in a world that is dead? The contemplation of that question alone should do much to stir our hearts towards the agenda of God.

Our world must be confronted; it has grown soft and comfortable. Paul continually confronted the sensual narcissistic generation in which he lived and yet not in a finger-pointing way. He was moved as much by the tragedy *of* the world, as the tragedy that existed in the world. Our confrontation must be mixed with true compassion. Our world surely needs both. It must be confronted with the error of its ways, the tragedy of giving itself to empty dreams. But that confrontation must come from a people committed to God's agenda, not just with their hearts but with their hands and feet, demonstrating in tangible ways the love and care of Jesus; giving people an opportunity to sense his heart. And along with compassionate confrontation, there must be confirmation of the value of every life. Jesus came for the marginalised and gave himself for the insignificant. That is what his followers must be about, affirming the true value and worth of people. It's about seeing people's value and usefulness to God beyond their immediate appearance.

There is a moment of incredible insight and tenderness in what is regarded as the Apostle Paul's last letter before his life was ended by the Romans. Writing from prison at the close of his life, he was reaching out to those whose day was just beginning. The letter was written to Timothy, his disciple, and the challenge of the letter was to call this young man and others to assume the torch of testimony for their generation. The challenge was not an easy one. The fact that Paul was writing from prison demonstrated the precariousness of following Jesus. Along with that, Paul wrote of the many obstacles both in and outside the church that would seek to hold them back. But towards the close of the letter there are

two words of incredible meaning: 'Get Mark' (2 Tim
4:11). Paul asked Timothy to come and visit him and
bring along this man Mark '. . . because he is helpful
to me in my ministry'. What is so remarkable about
this statement is that this is the same Mark who had
abandoned Barnabas and Paul in the early days of
their mission to the Gentiles. He was a young man,
who had lived all of his life in the shadow of the
early giants of the church. When Peter had been
miraculously released from prison it was to Mark's
mother's house that he went. But he had failed and
had caused a devisive rift between Barnabas and
Paul. Barnabas, the encourager, wanted to give
Mark another chance, but at that time Paul didn't
want a failure on his team. And yet at the end of
his life, he called for Mark and told Timothy
that he would be helpful, useful, to Paul and his
ministry. The implication in Paul's words was that
Mark was now responsive and he needed a man like
that.

We must also be responsive. If we encounter need
and cannot respond or empathise, then we are
surely missing the heart of God. Effective ministry is
not the glorious display of power and giftedness but
faithful service in the purposes of God. In this
generation that is so restless, so distracted, the love
of God needs to be affirmed.

Mother Teresa is regarded by many as a
twentieth-century saint—one who exemplifies the
nature of Jesus. Yet it is not for her theology that
she is so recognised. It is her incarnational
Christianity.

We live in a very dehumanising world. It seems
that people get used and abused on so many different levels. Lust, greed and selfishness transcend

true human characteristics of love, empathy and compassion. God has called us to be a community reflecting his passion for justice, righteousness and mercy. Our society follows that which is modelled to it. Rock stars become the role models for dress and attitude among teenagers. Sports fans wear their favourite player's brand of tennis shoes. Television and cinema set the trends for society's choices and values. In this kind of world, it's important that we model Jesus. 'For I have set you an example that you should do as I have done for you' (Jn 13:15).

As our world has released itself from moral absolutes, and truth has become relative, our societies are no longer producing men and women of great character. Integrity has become a thing of the past. Betrayal, backstabbing and lies have become socially acceptable means of achieving personal goals. We, then, must learn to deal with people with a deep level of biblical integrity. This involves preferring and honouring others, allowing our lives to be characterised by the seeming frailty of honesty. Like many other institutions, the church has seen more than its fair share of scandals and failings. In these times, the right of the church to be a voice to society is seriously challenged and questioned. To combat that, we must present purity of character, morality and unity. Also, in an age where care is lost, we must learn to communicate in a caring manner. As we said earlier, Jesus never allowed sin to stand in the way of his love. We can no longer stand on the street corner proclaiming judgement to the passing cars. We will have to engage our culture intelligently and present our faith with reason, insight and care.

18

A Time of Expectation

Not until God brings down the curtain on history, do we have the prerogative of abandoning it to final destruction and doom. While the hand of God in judgement remains suspended we have an evangelistic and missionary opportunity that is all the more urgent. How colossally rewarding it would be if like a thief on the cross someone was snatched from final judgement and doom because in those last moments an opportunity for decision was clearly articulated and powerfully presented (Carl F. Henry).

'Well, Doctor Livingstone, where are you ready to go now?' . . . 'I am ready to go anywhere provided it be forward' (David Livingstone).

Father, if Jesus exists, then how come he never lived here? (Sting, 'All this Time').

Again Jesus said, 'Peace be with you! As the Father has sent me, I am sending you' (Jn 20:21).

The present-day story of our world is one of stunning upheaval. Everything is altering: national boundaries, identities, ideologies and philosophies. The west has lost its biggest enemy. The eastern bloc is struggling to find its new path. There is talk of a new world order built on the relationship of nations committed to building a better world. It seems that we are in a time of transition and immense change. If ever there was a time for the people of God to make a strong appearance on the world scene it is now.

I sense a pulling forward by the Lord; a call to move on, to press on. In Isaiah 40, the Israelites were told to get ready, to prepare, because God was about to act in a new way. 'A voice of one calling: "In the desert prepare the way for the Lord; make straight in the wilderness a highway for our God"' (Is 40:3). By the prophet, God sent a message bringing hope of freedom to the nation. It was a call to freshness and newness; a promise from God that out of death, life would spring. They were challenged to clear the way—to remove the hindrances and prepare for the triumphal entry of the conquering King. It was a call to look forward and not to look back. Jesus continually gave his disciples vision for the future: 'Open your eyes and look at the fields! They are ripe for harvest' (Jn 4:35). Not only did he give them vision for the future of the world, but vision for their own lives. He didn't chain them to their past and constantly remind them that they were ignorant fishermen or corrupt tax collectors. He filled them with what he had called them to and gave them vision of what they could become. To Jesus, it wasn't important where they came from as much as who they were becoming. His vision was to create an army of servants who would faithfully and worshipfully serve him and live out the commands of his kingdom. A people who without reservation would devote their all to see his dreams fulfilled in their own lives and in the world.

Part of being a follower of Jesus is to have a concern for the future, not simply an escapist theology that looks for any way out of this world but, armed with the knowledge that the King will come like a thief in the night, work for his kingdom in the earth.

The Apostle Paul was a man held captive by his future. He had no time to look back and revel in his achievements or mourn over his failures. He realised that he had been taken hold of:

> . . . but I press on to take hold of that for which Christ Jesus took hold of me. Brothers, I do not consider myself yet to have taken hold of it. But one thing I do: Forgetting what is behind and straining towards what is ahead, I press on towards the goal to win the prize for which God has called me heavenwards in Christ Jesus (Phil 3:12–14).

Paul committed himself to his future. He saw himself as part of God's glorious plan that had swept through history, and he lived with a sense that his future was dictated by the hold that Jesus had upon his life. He lived by the vision that had arrested and captivated him on the road to Damascus. He had such a sense of God's hand upon him that he considered anything that happened to him in his life a light affliction. And this from a man who was whipped, ship-wrecked, imprisoned and stoned! His eye had caught hold of something eternal and he purposed to live to capacity. He was not content with a portion. He wanted it all and was willing to do everything within his power to see it come to pass. Many people have great dreams for their lives, but no dream will just happen—it takes perseverance and work in order for it to be realised.

I believe that we are a privileged generation of believers. We live at a time of great expectancy in our world. As we approach the millennium there is much talk in the world about what the twenty-first century will hold. History teaches that men have an almost inbuilt expectancy for change when centuries or millennia change. The opportunities for the church are endless, but it will take renewed consideration of Christ's hold upon our lives.

At the beginning of this book we looked at the idea pervading our society that one person cannot make a difference. King Saul doesn't receive too many accolades for his reign and yet there were moments of great power and anointing as he yielded his life to God. On one occasion Israel's enemies besieged Jabesh Gilead and the men of the city offered to make peace. The leader of the enemy forces agreed to make peace on the condition that all the men of Jabesh Gilead were willing to have their right eyes gouged out and bring disgrace on Israel. The men of the city asked for seven days to find help before they would submit to such a thing. In tears, the report was brought to Saul, who had been made king but actually was still farming because there wasn't much to be king over. When Saul heard the story, he became extremely angry and he took his oxen and cut them to pieces and sent messengers throughout Israel carrying pieces of raw flesh and telling all that what had happened to the oxen would be done to any man who did not heed the call to battle. Needless to say, there was a great response and 330,000 men showed up to protect Jabesh Gilead and put the enemy to flight (1 Sam 11). Israel was saved from disgrace and the men of that city from disfigurement because one man chose to do all he could to stem the tide of evil. This is another example of one man's actions, which not only united people, but also changed the circumstances of life. The Bible says that the power of God came upon Saul and caused him to be angry. God is looking for hearts willing to allow his passions to be manifested in them, that they may be raised up to stem the tide of evil.

While we may well question many aspects of Latin American theology, some of its insights are entirely accurate, not least the maxim: 'Where you stand determines what you see.' The view from the mountaintop is different from the view from the valley. After years of wandering in the wilderness, God took Moses to a higher place and showed him Israel's destiny. What a sight it must have been in Moses' eyes after all those years in the wilderness. After all those struggles to come to the very edge of the Land of Promise, he saw laid out before him the land which had once been but a dream to a nation of slaves with no hope or identity of their own.

Jesus did a lot of things on mountainsides. In response to the huge crowd gathered to hear him, he went up onto a mountainside and laid out the Sermon on the Mount. On a mountainside he met with Moses and Elijah in a moment full of God's power and glory. On a mountainside he called his disciples—those he not only needed for his purposes, but also wanted to have in his company. The disciples' life with Jesus began on a mountainside, and their earthly relationship with him ended in a similar place.

> Then the eleven disciples went to Galilee, to the mountain where Jesus had told them to go. When they saw him, they worshipped him; but some doubted. Then Jesus came to them and said, 'All authority in heaven and on earth has been given to me. Therefore go and make disciples of all nations, baptising them in the name of the Father and of the Son and of the Holy

Spirit, and teaching them to obey everything I have commanded you' (Mt 28:16–20).

Considering the events that had taken place during the days prior to this—the warmth and love of the Last Supper, the fear and disintegration of everything in the garden, the denials, the death and then the resurrection—as they climbed the mountainside there must have been a great sense of bewilderment as evidenced by the statement that some of them doubted. Jesus didn't even address the past; he simply, once again, gave them vision for the future. His statement was perhaps the most audacious ever made. There was no demand for a new religion—there was already a glut of them and there seemed to be no need for another religious thread to be woven into the world. Instead, Jesus gave these eleven his vision for the kingdom: that it would cover the whole earth. He sent them out because he wanted them to substitute his thinking for all existing religious thought. Sometime before, in the course of his teaching ministry, Jesus had likened the kingdom of heaven to the yeast that a woman took and mixed into a large amount of flour until it worked into all the dough. He had used that analogy to portray the seeming insignificance of the kingdom, and yet, in likening it to yeast, he was describing its tendency to expand its influence until it had penetrated and consumed everything. The kingdom and its King will not be satisfied until its influence has expanded to saturate and penetrate the whole earth.

He laid before those men the vision of the future kingdom, and he wrapped their destiny up with it. He called them to commit themselves to the future and gave them his dream for the nations of the earth. He called them to live with kingdom eyes; to be consumed with a vision for a world changed by his love. From that mountainside, Jesus ascended into glory, and the disciples went down the mountain and preached everywhere.

May we be willing to give all to follow in the footsteps of love, and with kingdom eyes have but one vision and one cry: 'Your kingdom come, your will be done on earth as it is in heaven.'

Notes

1. David Sweetman, *Van Gogh, His Life and Art* (Simon & Schuster, 1990).
2. Quoted in *Reader's Digest*, July 1990.
3. *ibid.*
4. Charles Birch, *Confronting the Future* (Penguin, 1976).
5. Naisbitt & Aburdene, *Megatrends 2000* (Pan, 1991).
6. Source unknown.
7. Quoted in *Christianity Today*, August 8, 1991.
8. Quoted in *Reader's Digest*.
9. Desmond Tutu, *The Words of Desmond Tutu* (Spire, 1989).
10. Quoted in Alan Walker, *Try God* (Lancer, 1990).
11. Bill Hybels, Stuart Briscoe & Haddon Robinson, *Mastering Contemporary Preaching* (Inter-Varsity, 1991).
12. Desmond Tutu, *op. cit.*
13. Quoted in A. E. Hotchner, *Blown Away* (Simon & Schuster, 1990).
14. Quoted in Kenneth E. Bailey, *Through Peasants' Eyes* (Eerdmans, 1976).
15. Don Henley, 'The Heart of the Matter' from *The End of the Innocence* (Geffen Records, 1989).

16. Ron Boehme, *Leadership for the 21st Century* (Frontline Communications, 1989).

17. Mike Stand, 'Footsteps of Love' from *Simple Expressions* (Frontline Records, 1990).

18. Kenneth E. Bailey, *op. cit.*

19. Quoted in *Journey to the Nations* (Caleb Project, 1983).

20. Joy Dawson, 'Ordinary Men and Women who Became Heroes of the Faith' (Pilgrim Tapes, 1986).

21. Ric Alba, 'Life Begins at the Cross' from *Gut Level Music* (Frontline Records, 1986).

22. Dietrich Bonhoeffer, *Cost of Discipleship* (SCM, 1964).

23. Quoted in Elisabeth Elliot, *Journals of Jim Elliot, Shadows of the Almighty.*

24. *Microsoft MS-DOS, User's Guide and User's Reference* (Microsoft Corporation, 1987, 1988).

25. Quoted in Frederick Douglass, *My Bondage and My Freedom* (Dover, 1970).

26. Howard Snyder, *The Radical Wesley* (IVP).